Microcomputer Applications for Business Series

MW00745616

AN INTRODUCTION TO

DOS

VERSIONS 5.0 / 6.0

Microcomputer Applications for Business Series

AN INTRODUCTION TO

DOS

VERSIONS 5.0 / 6.0

■　　　■　　　■

Harry L. Phillips
Santa Rosa Junior College

Course Technology, Inc. One Main Street, Cambridge, MA 02142

An Introduction to DOS Versions 5.0/6.0 is published by Course Technology, Inc.

Editorial Director	Joseph B. Dougherty
Product Manager	Nicole Jones
Production Manager	Myrna D'Addario
Production Editor	Robin M. Geller
Production Coordinator	Kathleen Finnegan
Production Assistant	Erin Bridgeford
Desktop Publishing Supervisor	Debbie Masi
Desktop Publishers	Tom Atwood
	Andy Giammarco
Copyeditor	Andrea Goldman
Proofreader	Jill L. Turnbull
Technical Review Specialist	Mark Vodnik
Student Reviewers	Jane Dougherty
	Jim Valente
Manufacturing Manager	Elizabeth Martinez
Print Buyer/Planner	Charlie Patsios
Cover Designer	Darci Mehall

An Introduction to DOS Versions 5.0/6.0 © 1993 by Course Technology, Inc.

Trademarks

Disclaimer

Course Technology, Inc. reserves the right to revise this publication and from time to time make changes in its content without notice.

ISBN 1-56527-067-3 (text and 3½-inch Data Disk)

Printed in the United States of America.
10 9 8 7 6 5 4 3 2 1

From the Publisher

At Course Technology, Inc., we believe that technology will transform the way that people teach and learn. We are very excited about bringing you, college professors and students, the most practical and affordable technology-related products available.

The Course Technology Development Process

Our development process is unparalleled in the higher education publishing industry. Every product we create goes through an exacting process of design, development, review, and testing.

Reviewers give us direction and insight that shape our manuscripts and bring them up to the latest standards. Every manuscript is quality tested. Students whose backgrounds match the intended audience work through every keystroke, carefully checking for clarity and pointing out errors in logic and sequence. Together with our own technical reviewers, these testers help us ensure that everything that carries our name is error-free and easy to use.

Course Technology Products

We show both *how* and *why* technology is critical to solving problems in college and in whatever field you choose to teach or pursue. Our time-tested, step-by-step instructions provide unparalleled clarity. Examples and applications are chosen and crafted to motivate students.

The Course Technology Team

This book will suit your needs because it was delivered quickly, efficiently, and affordably. In every aspect of our business, we rely on a commitment to quality and the use of technology. Every employee contributes to this process. The names of all of our employees are listed below:

Tom Atwood, Stephen M. Bayle, Josh Bernoff, Erin Bridgeford, Ann Marie Buconjic, Jody Buttafoco, Marcia Cole, Susan Collins, John M. Connolly, David Crocco, Myrna D'Addario, Lisa D'Alessandro, Tracy Day, Howard S. Diamond, Katie Donovan, Joseph B. Dougherty, MaryJane Dwyer, Don Fabricant, Robin M. Geller, Suzanne Goguen, Eileen Gorham, Roslyn Hooley, Nicole Jones, Matt Kenslea, Wendy Kincaid, Suzanne Licht, Elizabeth Martinez, Debbie Masi, Kathleen McCann, Mac Mendelsohn, Laurie Michelangelo, Kim Munsell, Paul Murphy, Amy Oliver, Debbie Parlee, Kristin Patrick, Charlie Patsios, Darren Perl, George J. Pilla, David Smith, Kathy Sutherland, Michelle Tucker, David Upton, Mark Valentine, Mark Vodnik, Jacqueline Winspear

■   ■   ■

Preface

An Introduction to DOS Versions 5.0/6.0 acclimates students to the DOS environment. The first part, "Essential Computer Concepts," presents an overview of computers and includes only those concepts that students need before they go into the lab. The three DOS tutorials give students step-by-step instructions on how to use DOS for file management in both diskette and hard disk environments. Both the concepts chapters and the DOS tutorials are unique in their approach. They motivate all of the concepts and skills they teach by explaining *why* students need to learn them.

The Textbook

An Introduction to DOS Versions 5.0/6.0 includes the following features in each DOS tutorial:

Objectives   A list of objectives orients students to the goals of each tutorial.

Tutorial Case   This case presents a business problem that students could reasonably encounter on the job. Thus, the process of solving the problem will be meaningful to students.

Step-by-Step Methodology   This unique methodology integrates concepts and keystrokes. Students are asked to press keys always within the context of solving the problem. The text constantly guides students, letting them know *why* they are pressing the keys.

Page Design   Each page is designed to help students easily differentiate between what they are to *do* and what they are to *read*. In addition, the numerous screen shots include labels that direct students' attention to what they should look at on the screen.

Exercises   The tutorials conclude with meaningful, conceptual questions that test students' understanding of what they learned in the tutorial.

Tutorial Assignments   These assignments provide students with additional practice on the individual DOS skills that they learned in the tutorial. Students practice by modifying the problems that they solved in the tutorial and by working on new problems.

The Supplements

Data Disk

The Data Disk includes all the files needed to complete the tutorials and the Tutorial Assignments. It is available in 3½-inch format. (If you need a 5¼-inch diskette, see your instructor.)

Instructor's Manual

The instructor's manual is written by the author and is quality assured. It includes:

- Answers and solutions to the Exercises and Tutorial Assignments
- A 3½-inch diskette containing solutions to the Tutorial Assignments
- Transparency masters of key figures in the tutorials, selected by the author

Test Bank

This supplement contains approximately 50 questions per tutorial in true/false, multiple choice, matching, and short answer formats. Each question has been tested by students for accuracy and clarity.

Electronic Test Bank

The Electronic Test Bank allows instructors to edit individual test questions, select questions individually or at random, and print out scrambled versions of the same test to any supported printer.

Acknowledgments

I especially wish to thank the dedicated staff of Course Technology for their invaluable professional contributions to this book. Nicole Jones, Product Manager, enthusiastically managed the direction and development of this book and contributed many valuable ideas for improving its quality and focus. Joe Dougherty, Editorial Director, and Katherine Pinard, Product Manager, initiated this project and contributed to the original direction of this book. Mark Vodnik, Technical Review Specialist, directed the extensive testing of each tutorial. Mark Vodnik, Jane Dougherty, and Jim Valente thoroughly tested and evaluated the book from the standpoint of the student and offered valuable suggestions for improving and integrating the presentation of information. I thank Myrna D'Addario, Production Manager; Robin Geller, Production Editor; Kathleen Finnegan, Production Coordinator; Erin Bridge-ford, Production Assistant; Debbie Masi, Desktop Publishing Supervisor; Tom Atwood and Andy Giammarco, Desktop Publishers; Andrea Goldman, Copyeditor; Jill Turnbull, Proofreader; Elizabeth Martinez, Manufacturing Manager; Charlie Patsios, Manufacturing and Package Designer; and Darci Mehall, Cover Designer, for their special expertise and contributions to the book. I thank David Crocco, Product Manager, for discussing the possibility of my participation in this project.

I wish to thank John Connolly for creating an exciting, innovative company with a strong commitment to the development of high-quality textbooks. His vision continues to have a significant impact on the education of college students throughout the United States.

The reviewers of this textbook — Jerold Jacobs of Penn Valley Community College, William Leedy of Wilmington College, Dianne Maricle of Diablo Valley College, and John Zales of Harrisburg Area Community College — offered constructive and critical ideas and suggestions on the focus and coverage of this textbook and deserve special thanks for their efforts.

Once again, I thank my many friends, colleagues, co-workers, family, and parents for their unending belief in what I have to offer and how I offer it.

Harry L. Phillips

Brief Contents

Table of Contents

Essential Computer Concepts

■   ■   ■

Essential Computer Concepts

What Is a Computer?

Computers have become prominent tools in almost every type of activity in virtually every type of business (Figure 1). What exactly is this important business tool? By definition, a **computer** is an electronic device that can perform operations — such as mathematical calculations or comparisons of numbers and characters — at extremely high speeds. But this definition fails to convey the power and the influence of computers in today's society. Computers can organize and process **data** (information of any kind — numbers, words, formulas, and so forth), manage financial information, create and manipulate graphics, and perform many other tasks to help business personnel be more efficient and productive.

Figure 1: Office workers at their computers

OBJECTIVES

In this chapter you will learn to:

- Define and describe a computer

- Distinguish among a microcomputer, minicomputer, mainframe, and supercomputer

- Describe the major components of computer hardware

- Describe the functions of common input and output devices

- List the sizes and capacities of common storage media

- Describe the major types of computer software, including systems software and applications software

Types of Computers

Figure 2:   A microcomputer

Computers are often classified by their size, speed, and cost. **Microcomputers**, also called **personal computers**, are inexpensive enough — $500 to $15,000 — for individuals to own and small enough to fit on an office desk (Figure 2). Some microcomputers are so small they can fit comfortably on your lap; appropriately they are called **laptop computers** (Figure 3). Other microcomputers, called **notebook computers**, are small enough to fit easily into a briefcase (Figure 4).

You'll probably use microcomputers throughout college and throughout your business career. Microcomputers are used extensively in small and large businesses. But some large businesses, government agencies, and other institutions also use larger and faster types of computers. One of these larger and faster computers is the **minicomputer** (Figure 5). Minicomputers are too large and too heavy for desktops, run three to 25 times faster than microcomputers, and cost anywhere from $15,000 to $500,000.

Figure 3:   A laptop computer

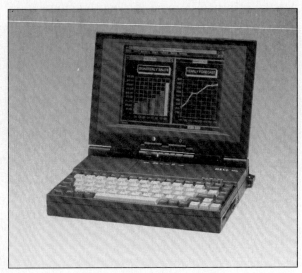

Figure 4:   A notebook computer

Figure 5: A minicomputer

A still larger and more powerful computer is the **mainframe computer** (Figure 6). Mainframes have large capacities for storing and manipulating data, run 10 to 100 times faster than a microcomputer, and cost anywhere from $100,000 to $2 million.

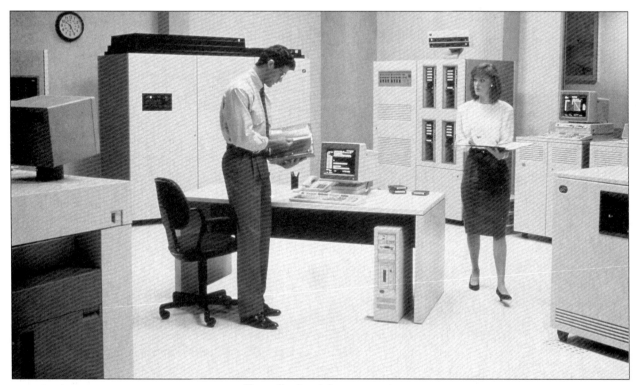

Figure 6: A mainframe computer

Figure 7: A Cray supercomputer

The largest and fastest computers, called **supercomputers**, are so large and expend so much energy that they require their own internal cooling systems to dissipate the heat generated during their operation (Figure 7). Supercomputers are so expensive, often costing several million dollars, that only the largest companies, government agencies, and universities can afford them. Typically supercomputers run 50 to 10,000 times faster than a microcomputer.

With the accelerated development of new and better computers, the guidelines for classifying types of computers have become fuzzy. For example, some recently developed microcomputers run at higher speeds than some minicomputers. Since this book focuses on microcomputers, subsequent discussions will deal primarily with microcomputers. Most of the concepts, however, apply equally well to larger, more powerful computers.

Computer Hardware

The components of a computer that you can see and touch are often collectively called **hardware**. They include the monitor (the TV-like screen), the keyboard, the disk drives, the printer, and the part of the computer that does most of the work.

Computer hardware typically is divided into four categories: input devices, processing hardware, output devices, and storage media (Figure 8). These categories reflect the activities that the computer hardware performs. Suppose, for example, that you wanted to use the computer to write a letter. You would use the keyboard (an input device) to put the words of your letter into the processing hardware, which is found inside the main computer. Once inside the processing hardware, your words would be manipulated to form lines of the appropriate width and pages of the appropriate length and be centered, underlined, or italicized according to your instructions. After you finished your letter, you would use the printer (an output device) to reproduce the letter on paper. Finally, you would save a copy of your letter on a disk (a storage medium) for future reference.

Since you have to use input devices, processing hardware, and output devices for every task you want to perform on a computer, let's discuss each of these components in more detail.

Input Devices

Data entered into the computer are called **input**. The hardware involved in sending input to the computer is called an **input device**. The two most common microcomputer input devices are a **keyboard** and a **mouse**.

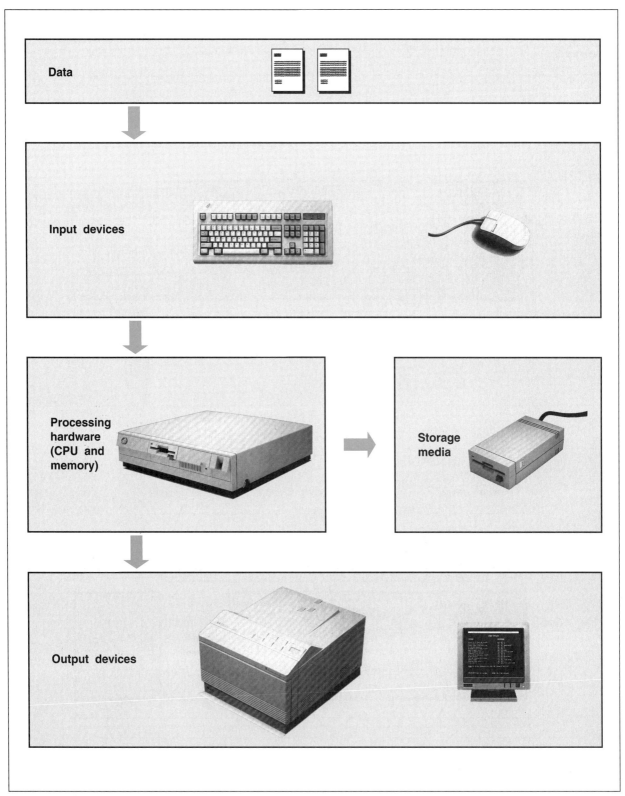

Figure 8: The relationship among input devices, processing hardware, output devices, and storage media

Most of the keys on your computer keyboard work just like the keys on a typewriter. Some features of a computer keyboard, however, are unique to computers. Figure 9 shows the standard 83-key IBM PC-style keyboard, and Figure 10 shows the enhanced 101-key IBM PS/2-style keyboard.

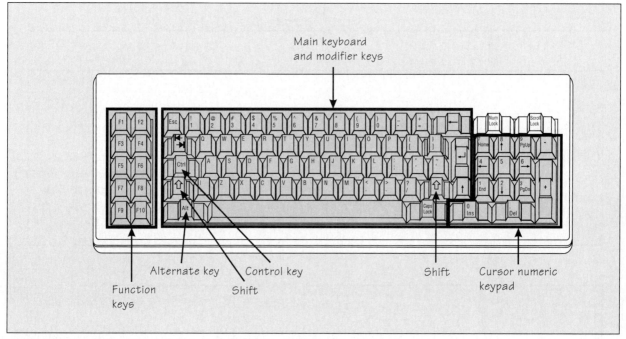

Figure 9: Standard 83-key keyboard

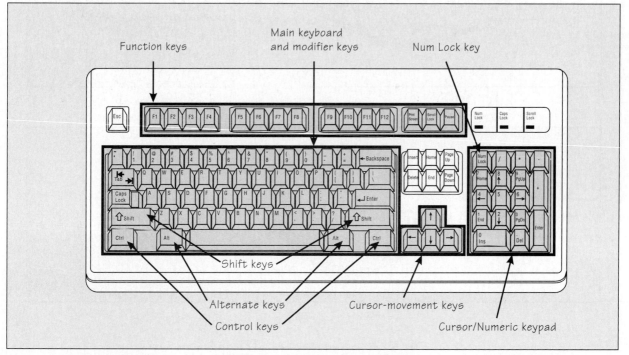

Figure 10: Enhanced 101-key keyboard

The computer keyboards in Figures 9 and 10 consist of three major parts:

- Main keyboard and modifier keys
- Cursor/numeric keypad
- Function keys

The **main keyboard** works like the keys on an electric typewriter. To type text, you just press the keys. To type uppercase letters or symbols such as ~, !, @, #, and $, you press the [Shift] key (a modifier key) and while holding it down, press the desired keyboard letter or symbol key, then release both keys. In addition, you can combine the [Shift] key, the alternate key, [Alt], and the control key, [Ctrl], with other keystrokes to accomplish special tasks, such as saving or printing data.

The **cursor/numeric keypad** on both the standard and the enhanced keyboards is located to the right of the main keyboard. Turn [Num Lock] off (the [Num Lock] key is located just above the numeric keypad), and you can use the keypad to move the **cursor**, a blinking underscore character (_) or a rectangle that marks where the next character that you type will appear on the screen. Turn [Num Lock] on, and you can use the keypad to type numbers and other special symbols, such as the decimal point, the plus sign, and the minus sign.

Enhanced keyboards contain a separate set of cursor-movement keys between the main keyboard and the keypad. Thus, you can leave [Num Lock] on and use the numeric keypad to enter numbers and the cursor-movement keys to move the cursor.

The **function keys** are located to the left of the main keyboard on a standard keyboard and above the main keyboard on an enhanced keyboard. You use the function keys alone or with the modifier keys ([Shift], [Alt], and [Ctrl]) to execute special tasks, such as saving or printing data.

Your computer system may also be equipped with a **mouse** (Figure 11). As you push or pull the mouse along a surface, such as your desk, a **mouse pointer** moves on the monitor screen. A mouse allows you to position the cursor anywhere on the screen and to execute certain commands. Sometimes you can accomplish tasks more efficiently by using a mouse than by using a keyboard.

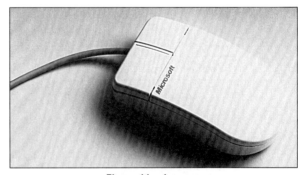

Figure 11: A mouse

Processing Hardware

The most important hardware elements within a computer are the **central processing unit (CPU)**, or **microprocessor** — sometimes called the "brains" of the computer — and the **memory**, which stores instructions and data in the computer. Although you usually don't have to think consciously about the CPU and the memory while you are using a computer, you should be aware of the different types and speeds of microprocessors. Knowing about the different memory capacities of computers is helpful in case you want to buy your own computer or have to help decide what computers to buy in your business.

Figure 12: An Intel 80386 microprocessor, the CPU found in many IBM-compatible computers

The most popular microprocessors in IBM personal computers and IBM-compatible computers — those that run like IBM computers — are the Intel 8088, 8086, 80286, 80386, and 80486 (Figure 12). The numbers are simply model numbers designated by the manufacturer. Generally speaking the higher the number, the more powerful the microprocessor, meaning the microprocessor can handle more data at a time and faster.

The speed of a microprocessor is determined by its **clock rate**. The computer clock is part of a group of circuits associated with the CPU. Think of the clock rate as the "heartbeat" or "pulse" of the computer. The higher the clock rate, the faster the computer. Clock rate is measured in millions of cycles per second, or **megahertz (MHz)**. The Intel 8088 microprocessor on the first IBM PC ran at only 4.77 MHz; the Intel 80486 microprocessor on some current machines runs at 50 MHz.

The computer memory is a set of storage locations in the main part of the computer. Computers store instructions and data by using microscopic electronic switches, which can be either on or off. By associating an on switch with the number 1 and an off switch with the number 0, we can represent computer data with **binary** or **base-2** numbers, which consist of binary digits (called **bits**) with the value 0 or 1.

Computers generally store data in groups of eight bits, called **bytes**. A byte representing the integer value 0 is 00000000, with all eight bits set to 0; a byte representing the integer value 1 is 00000001; and a byte representing the integer value 2 is 00000010. Figure 13 shows the binary representation of some of the integer numbers from 0 through 255.

Each byte can also represent a character, such as A or @. For example, in IBM-compatible microcomputers an A is represented by the byte 01000001, B by 01000010, and C by 01000011. The characters ! (exclamation point), . (period), and + (plus sign) are represented by 00100001, 00101110, and 00101011, respectively.

Byte values can represent not only integers and characters, but also other types of data or instructions. A computer can determine the difference between the various types of data or instructions based on the context of the byte value, just as you can tell, based on the context, the difference between the two meanings of the word "hit" in the sentences "He hit me in the arm" and "The movie was a big hit."

As a computer user, you don't have to know the binary representation of numbers, characters, and instructions, since the computer handles all the necessary conversions internally. However, because the amount of memory in a computer and the storage capacity of disks are expressed in bytes, you should be aware of how data are stored so you will understand the capacity and the limitations of your computer.

Number	Binary representation
0	00000000
1	00000001
2	00000010
3	00000011
4	00000100
5	00000101
6	00000110
7	00000111
8	00001000
:	:
14	00001110
15	00001111
16	00010000
17	00010001
:	:
253	11111101
254	11111110
255	11111111

Figure 13: Binary representation of the numbers 0 through 255

For example, most IBM-compatible microcomputers have 640K (K means **kilobytes**) or 1MB (MB means **megabytes**) of memory. The prefix *kilo-* means one thousand, but for historical and technical reasons, a kilobyte is actually 1,024 bytes. The prefix *mega-* usually means one million, but in computer terms it literally means 1,024 x 1,024, or 1,048,576. A 640K computer can hold the equivalent of 640 x 1,024, or 655,360, characters. A 1MB computer can hold the equivalent of 1,048,576 characters, which approximately equals the amount of text in a 400-page book.

Memory comprises two types: read-only memory and random access memory. **Read-only memory**, or **ROM**, is the part of memory reserved for special data that are required for the internal workings of the computer. The microprocessor can read these data,

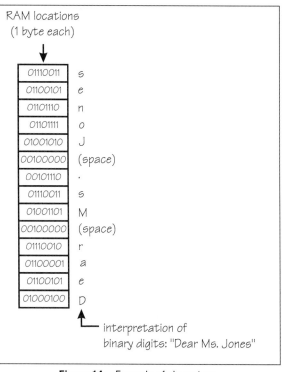

Figure 14: Example of characters stored in RAM

but it cannot erase or change the data. When you turn off your computer, the data in ROM remain intact, ready for use when you turn the computer back on.

Random-access memory, or **RAM**, is memory that is available to store input and processed information. A computer's microprocessor can read data from and write data to any location in RAM at any time. For example, when you type a report on your computer, the microprocessor stores the characters (letters, numbers, and so forth) of your report in RAM (Figure 14). When you modify the report, the microprocessor saves the new version in RAM. When you turn off your computer, the information in RAM is lost. Therefore, before turning off your computer, you need to save your work to a more permanent data storage medium.

Computer hardware also consists of ports and slots. **Ports** are the electronic pathways that pass data between the computer's CPU and its peripherals. **Peripherals** are hardware components, such as printers and monitors, that are connected to the main part of the computer. Microcomputers have two types of ports: serial and parallel (Figure 15). **Serial ports** send information between the CPU and other computer components one bit at a time. **Parallel ports** send information as multiple bits,

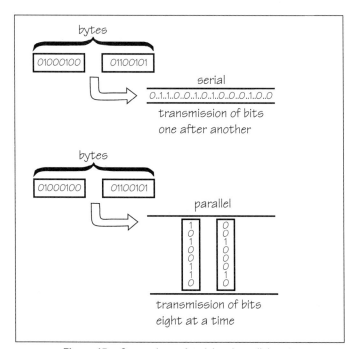

Figure 15: Comparison of serial and parallel ports

usually eight bits (one byte) at a time. Computer printers are often designated as serial or parallel to indicate the type of port to which they connect. Serial printers are usually connected to the port called **COM1** or **COM2** (for COMmunications port 1 or 2), and parallel printers are usually connected to the port called **LPT1** or **LPT2** (for Line PrinTer port 1 or 2). You need to know about these ports if you ever have to set up your own computer.

When you buy a printer or any other peripheral, make sure your computer has the right kind of port to match the peripheral. For example, if a new laser printer requires a serial port, make sure your computer has an available serial port to which you can connect the printer. If it doesn't, you can buy and install a board (or add-in card) that contains one or more additional ports. A **board**, or an **add-in card**, is a rectangular plate with electronic circuitry that you can insert into a slot. **Slots** are electrical connectors inside the computer (Figure 16). For example, one slot might contain a board that provides a serial port for a printer, as shown in Figure 16.

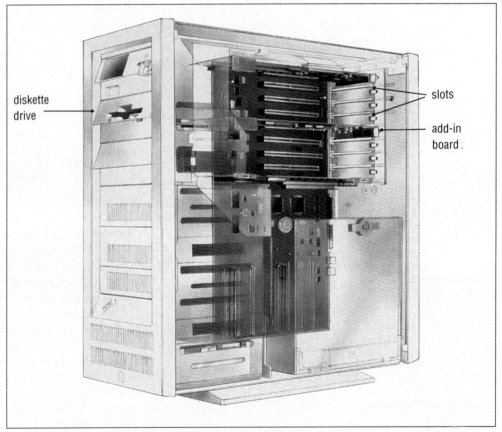

diskette drive

slots

add-in board

Figure 16: Slots in a vertically-configured microcomputer

Another slot might contain a board that allows the computer to communicate with other computers through a telephone line.

Output Devices

After you send data to the computer through an input device and after the CPU processes the data, the computer sends the processed data to a peripheral for storage or display. Data sent from the computer to the peripheral are called **output**, and the storage or display peripheral is called an **output device**. The most commonly used output devices are monitors and printers.

A **monitor** is the TV-like video screen that displays the output from a computer (Figure 17). Most microcomputers use a **CRT** (cathode ray tube) as the monitor screen. Most laptop computers use a flat-panel display, such as an **LCD** (liquid crystal display).

The text and graphics displayed on computer monitors are created with little dots of light called **pixels** (short for "picture elements") (Figure 18). Each pixel on a monochrome monitor has only one color (green, amber, or white) when the pixel is on and no color (black)

Figure 17: A color monitor

when the pixel is off. Each pixel on a color monitor, on the other hand, can appear in any of several colors.

The entire monitor screen is a grid of pixels that combine to create the illusion of a continuous image. For example, a **CGA** (color graphics adaptor) monitor has a 320 x 200 grid, that is, 320 pixels horizontally and 200 pixels vertically. A **VGA** (video graphics array) monitor has a 640 x 480 grid. The higher the number of pixels on a monitor, the clearer and sharper the graphics images it can display.

IBM-compatible monitors have two modes: text and graphics. In **text mode**, the monitor can display only text — letters, digits, and special characters. In **graphics mode**, the monitor can display graphic images as well as text. All monitors have a text mode, but not all monitors have a graphics mode.

A **printer** produces a paper copy of the text or graphics processed by the computer. A paper copy of computer output is called **hard copy**, because it is more tangible and permanent than the electronic or magnetic copies found on a disk, in the computer memory, or on the monitor.

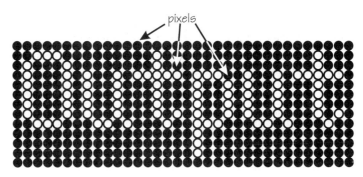

Figure 18

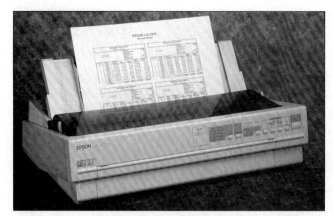

Figure 19: A dot-matrix printer

This is sample output from a
24-pin dot-matrix printer
in DRAFT mode

This is sample output from a
24-pin dot-matrix printer
in NLQ mode

Figure 20:   Sample output from a dot-matrix printer

The three most popular types of printers are dot-matrix, ink-jet, and laser printers. **Dot-matrix printers** form images by producing tiny dots of ink on the printer paper (Figure 19). The dots are formed when pins strike an inked ribbon. Less expensive dot-matrix printers have nine pins. More expensive models have 24 pins and produce higher-quality output. Figure 20 shows the text output from a 24-pin dot-matrix printer in draft mode. **Draft mode** prints very quickly but produces relatively low-quality output. Figure 20 also shows text printed in **near letter-quality mode** (**NLQ**), which prints more slowly but produces higher-quality output.

Ink-jet printers spurt tiny dots of ink onto the paper to form text or graphics (Figure 21). Most ink-jet printers are faster than dot-matrix printers. They produce graphics of reasonable quality and text of high quality.

Laser printers use a laser beam to bond a black powdery substance, called **toner**, to the paper. This produces the highest-quality text and graphics of any type of printer (Figure 22). Moreover, laser printers are faster and quieter than dot-matrix and ink-jet printers. Laser printers can usually create output in several type styles (the appearance of the characters; for example, italics) and type sizes (the size of the characters) (Figure 23). For these reasons, laser printers are becoming the standard type of printer in the business world.

Figure 21: An ink-jet printer

Figure 22: A laser printer

This is Courier.

This is Times Roman.

This is Helvetica.

This is Bookman.

Figure 23: Sample output from a laser printer showing four typefaces in different font sizes

A **disk drive** is actually classified as both an input and an output device because it can send data to and receive data from the CPU (Figure 24). A disk drive helps the computer store data. Think of a disk drive as storing data in a manner similar to a tape recorder storing sound, except that instead of winding a tape, the disk drive spins a disk.

Storage Media

When you turn off your computer, you lose the information in the computer's RAM. For example, suppose you were typing the names, addresses, and other relevant data of the clients for a large company. As you typed, the computer would store this data in RAM. But how would you save these data for future use? You would store the data on a more permanent storage medium (Figure 25 on the next page). The most common storage media for microcomputers are diskettes and hard disks.

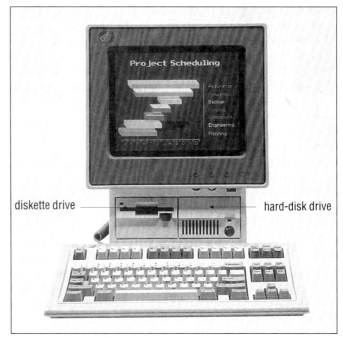

diskette drive

hard-disk drive

Figure 24: Disk drives in a computer

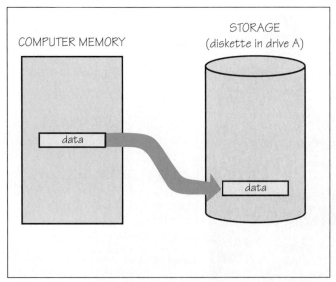

Figure 25: Storing data on a disk

Sometimes called **floppy disks**, **diskettes** are made of flat, circular, oxide-coated plastic enclosed in a square case called a **disk jacket**. The most common sizes of diskettes for microcomputers are 5¼ inches and 3½ inches (Figure 26). The 5¼-inch diskettes have soft, flexible disk jackets and are usually stored in paper sleeves for protection. The 3½-inch diskettes have hard plastic cases and don't require sleeves.

The most common types of diskettes are double-sided, double-density (DS/DD) and double-sided, high-density (DS/HD). The 5¼-inch DS/DD diskettes have a capacity of 360K, and the 3½-inch DS/DD diskettes have a capacity of 720K. The 5¼-inch DS/HD diskettes have a capacity of 1.2MB. The 3½-inch DS/HD diskettes have a capacity of 1.44MB.

Diskette drives are also available in double-density and high-density types. A high-density diskette drive can read from both high-density and double-density diskettes. A double-density diskette drive, on the other hand, can read only double-density diskettes. Before you purchase diskettes, make sure they match your diskette drive. For example, if you have a 3½-inch high-density diskette drive, you should generally buy and use only 3½-inch DS/HD diskettes. Usually you cannot distinguish between DD and HD diskettes just by looking at them. High-density diskettes sometimes have "HD" written on their cases; usually, however, you have to rely on the information printed on the packaging.

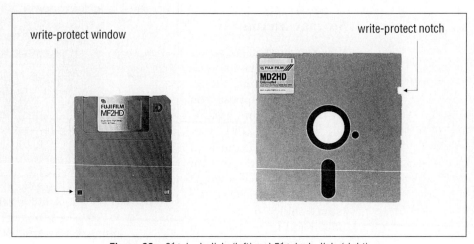

Figure 26: 3½-inch disk *(left)* and 5¼-inch disk *(right)*

Sometimes after you store information on a diskette, you may want to make sure that no one writes more information onto the diskette or erases the information from the diskette. For this purpose, diskettes provide **write protection**, which serves as a safeguard against losing valuable information. To write-protect a 5¼-inch diskette, you attach a write-protect tab across the write-protect notch; to write-protect a 3½-inch diskette, you open the write-protect window (Figure 27).

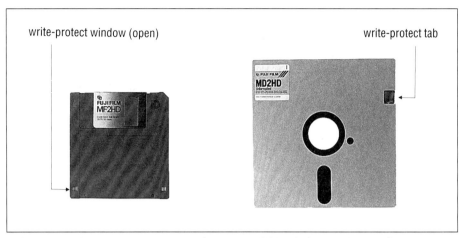

Figure 27:   Write-protected 3½-inch disk *(left)* and 5¼-inch disk *(right)*

Hard disks, also called **fixed disks**, are nonremovable, oxide-covered metal disks, usually mounted permanently within the computer. Hard disks have two advantages over diskettes: speed and capacity. The speed of a hard disk is measured by its **access time**, that is, the time required to read or write a byte of data. A typical hard disk has access times one-third to one-tenth those of a floppy disk; therefore, a hard disk is 3 to 10 times faster at accessing data.

The capacity of a hard disk is measured in megabytes (MB). A small hard disk with a capacity of 20MB can store the equivalent of about 8,000 pages of text, compared to only about 150 pages of text on a 360K 5¼-inch floppy disk. Most microcomputer hard disks have capacities in the range of 20MB to 400MB. These high capacities are more than just conveniences; much of the work currently performed by businesses using microcomputers requires these higher-capacity hard disks.

Networks

In the business world you usually don't work alone but rather as part of a team. As a team member, you'll probably use a **network**, a collection of connected computers and peripherals. A network allows you to share data and equipment with other members of the team.

Typically one of the computers on a network is equipped with a high-capacity hard drive and is designated as the **file server**, that is, it "serves" the data to the other computers and peripherals on the network. The most common type of network involving microcomputers is a local-area network. In a **local-area network** (**LAN**), computers are joined by direct cable links and are located relatively close to each other, for example, in the same building (Figure 28 on the next page). Each computer in the LAN has a special network board inserted into one of its slots, and each board is joined by an electrical cable to the file server. Other computer equipment, such as laser printers, may similarly be joined to the LAN. Many businesses use a LAN so groups of workers can share resources.

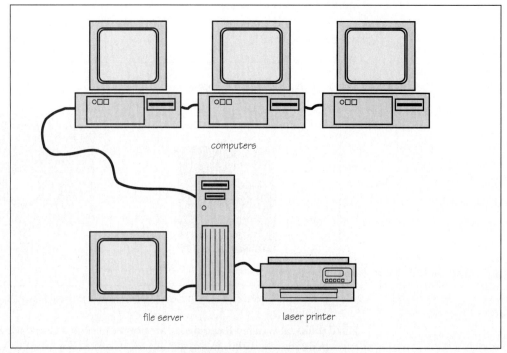

Figure 28: A local-area network

Computer Software

Just as a tape recorder or a compact disc player would be worthless without tapes or compact discs, computer hardware would be worthless without computer software. Software, also called **computer programs**, is sets of instructions that tell the computer what to do (Figure 29). The types of software that you use determine what you can do with your computer. For example, word processing software lets you use a computer to prepare documents, and graphics software lets you use a computer to create graphs and illustrations. Software can be divided into two general types: systems software and applications software.

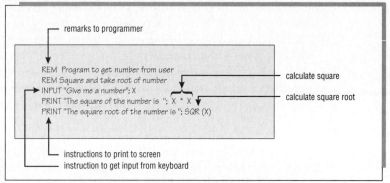

Figure 29: A computer program written in the
BASIC programming language

Systems Software

Systems software includes the programs that run the fundamental operations within your computer, such as starting the computer, loading programs and data into memory, executing programs, saving data to a disk, displaying information on the monitor screen, sending information through a port to a peripheral, and performing many other basic functions.

A special type of systems software is the **operating system**, which works like an air-traffic controller to coordinate the activities within a computer, including all the input and output operations to and from the peripherals. The most popular operating system for IBM-compatible microcomputers is **DOS** (rhymes with "boss"), for Disk Operating System. PC-DOS is marketed by IBM; the PC stands for Personal Computer. MS-DOS is marketed by Microsoft Corporation; hence, the abbreviation MS. Both systems were developed primarily by Microsoft Corporation and work in essentially the same way. Another systems software program developed by Microsoft is **Windows**, a graphics-based operating environment designed for ease of learning and ease of use.

Applications Software

A wide variety of software exists to help you accomplish many tasks on your computer. This type of software is called **applications software** because it allows you to *apply* your computer to accomplish specific goals. The four major types of applications software for business are word processing, spreadsheets, database management, and graphics.

Word processing software allows you to electronically create, edit, format, and print documents (Figure 30). The advantages of a word processor over a typewriter are numerous. With a word processor, you can move and delete text, check spelling, create tables and columns, modify margins, draw lines, change the appearance of text (to boldfaced or underlined, for example), and view how a document will appear *before* you print it. A word processor

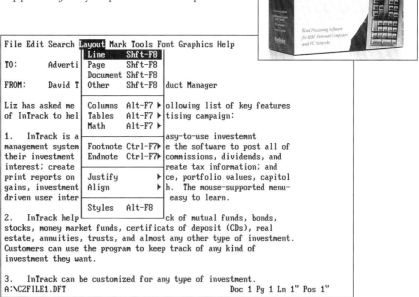

Figure 30: Example of a memo being produced with WordPerfect software and its pull-down menus

simplifies the process of printing headers, footers, page numbers, footnotes, endnotes, and line numbers. With a word processor, you don't have to worry about lines of text running into the margin, footnotes running off the bottom of the page, or titles being off-center. Word processing software takes care of these problems almost automatically.

An **electronic spreadsheet** allows you to perform calculations on numbers arranged in a grid of rows and columns on the computer screen (Figure 31). You can enter numbers, labels, formulas, and other kinds of information into the spreadsheet and automatically calculate the results. By using appropriate data and formulas, you can use an electronic spreadsheet to prepare financial reports and statements, analyze investment portfolios, calculate amortization tables, project income, and prepare a payroll, as well as perform many other tasks involved in making informed business decisions.

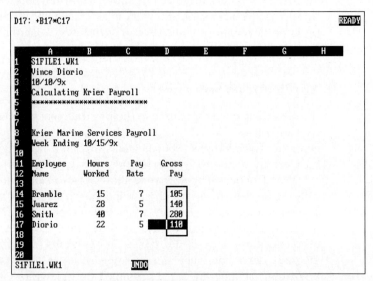

Figure 31:   Example of a spreadsheet created with Lotus 1-2-3 software

Database software helps you manage and manipulate information in the form of records, for example, information about employees, clients, schedules, supplies, equipment, or catalog entries (Figure 32). Database software allows you to easily retrieve, search, sort, select, delete, organize, and update a collection of data.

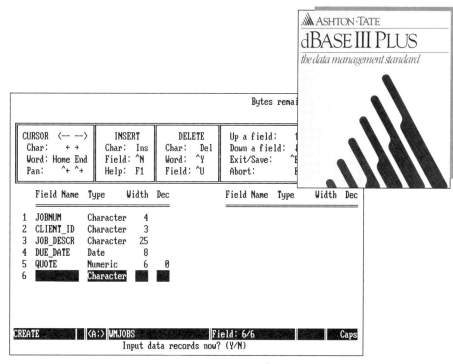

Figure 32: Example of a database file created with dBASE III PLUS software

Graphics software allows you to create illustrations, diagrams, graphs, and charts (Figure 33). For example, you could use graphics software to create a pie chart showing the major categories of expenses in your monthly budget. Most graphics software allows you to draw lines, boxes, circles, arrows, and other images; mix text and graphics; and enter raw data to create charts and graphs, as well as perform other operations to help prepare graphics as part of your business presentations, reports, and newsletters.

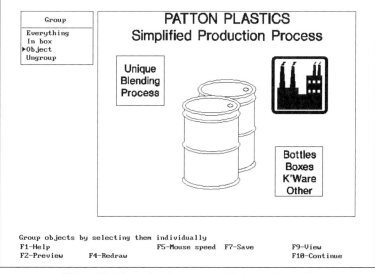

Figure 33: Example of a screen created using Harvard Graphics from Software Publishing Corporation

■   ■   ■

Exercises

1. Define or describe the following:
   a. hardware
   b. software
   c. cursor
   d. clock rate
   e. pixel

2. List and describe the four major classifications of computers based on their cost and speed.

3. What is the difference between a serial port and a parallel port?

4. Fill in the empty boxes in the following table with the storage capacities in kilobytes (K) or megabytes (MB) of each size of computer diskette:

	5¼-inch diskettes	3½-inch diskettes
DS/DD		
DS/HD		

5. Describe the two types of memory used by microcomputers.

6. Name the four major types of applications software used in business.

7. Describe each of the following hardware items:
   a. microprocessor
   b. slot
   c. port
   d. keyboard
   e. mouse
   f. monitor
   g. diskette drive

8. How would you write-protect a 5¼-inch diskette? A 3½-inch diskette? What is the purpose of write-protecting a diskette?

9. List the three most popular types of printers.

10. What is a network? What is the advantage of networking computers in business?

11. What is a network file server?

Photography Credits for *Essential Computer Concepts*

Figure	Credit	Page
1	Courtesy of International Business Machines	EC 3
2	Courtesy of International Business Machines	EC 4
3	Courtesy of Toshiba America Information Systems, Inc.	EC 4
4	Courtesy of Dell Computer Corporation	EC 4
5	Courtesy of International Business Machines	EC 5
6	Courtesy of International Business Machines	EC 5
7	Photo by Paul Shambroom, courtesy of Cray Research, Inc.	EC 6
8 keyboard	Courtesy of International Business Machines	EC 7
mouse	Courtesy of Microsoft Corporation	EC 7
CPU	Courtesy of International Business Machines	EC 7
disk drive	Courtesy of International Business Machines	EC 7
printer	Photo courtesy of Hewlett-Packard Company	EC 7
monitor	Courtesy of I-O Corporation	EC 7
11	Courtesy of Microsoft Corporation	EC 9
12	Courtesy of Intel Corporation	EC 10
16	Courtesy of International Business Machines	EC 12
17	Courtesy of NEC Technologies, Inc.	EC 13
19	Courtesy of Epson America, Inc.	EC 14
21	Photo courtesy of Hewlett-Packard Company	EC 14
22	Photo courtesy of Hewlett-Packard Company	EC 15
24	Courtesy of International Business Machines	EC 15
26	Richard Morgenstein	EC 16
27	Richard Morgenstein	EC 16
30	WordPerfect is a registered trademark of WordPerfect Corporation.	EC 19
31	Courtesy of Lotus Development Corporation	EC 20
33	The Harvard Graphics® package photo is used with the permission of Software Publishing Corporation, which owns the copyright to such product. Harvard Graphics® is a registered trademark of Software Publishing Corporation. Harvard Graphics® is a product of Software Publishing Corporation and has no connection with Harvard University.	EC 21

Essential Computer Concepts Index

DOS v5.0/6.0 Tutorials

- **Tutorial 1   Understanding DOS**

- **Tutorial 2   Working with Files**

- **Tutorial 3   Using Directories**

Tutorial 1

Understanding DOS

You have taken the leap and purchased a new computer system! You already plan a wide variety of uses for it. From your initial research, you learned that you can use the computer to prepare presentation-quality documents, develop a personal budget, keep personal and business records, build computer skills, and even play games. You will be able to work smarter and streamline time-consuming tasks that you once did by hand.

The salesperson points out that you will need to invest some time preparing yourself to use your new computer system. You must become familiar with the hardware as well as the different types of software included with your computer system. This initial investment in time will pay off in increased productivity and confidence in using your computer. Furthermore, you will be able to make important changes to your computer system, such as installing new software. You will also be able to troubleshoot problems.

After arriving home with your new computer system, you follow the instructions for getting started and set up the computer system within half an hour. You examine the reference materials and manuals provided with the computer and quickly discover that one of the most important types of software that you will use is operating system software.

OBJECTIVES

In this tutorial you will learn to:

- Identify the role of operating system software

- Identify files and filenames

- Identify drive, directory, and path names

- Start a computer system

- Identify the DOS version

- Set the date and time

- Use [F3] and DOSKEY to recall commands

- Clear the screen

- Use DOS Help

- Print a screen

- Format a diskette

- Make a copy of a diskette

- Turn off a computer system

What Is the Role of Operating System Software?

Operating system software is responsible for managing the basic processes required of a computer system. For example, the operating system handles all input and output operations. As you type, the operating system interprets the keys that you press on the keyboard and then displays the corresponding characters on the monitor. The operating system also interprets commands that you enter from the keyboard. If you enter a command to use an applications program, the operating system locates the program instructions on disk. Then, it copies those program instructions into the computer's memory so that you can use that software. When you issue a command to the applications program to save a document, the operating system stores a permanent copy of the document on the hard disk or on a diskette. If you want to print a copy of the document, the operating system transfers data from the computer system to the printer.

In these situations, the operating system coordinates the interaction of hardware and software in the computer system. It functions like the manager of an assembly line in an automobile factory. Each worker on the assembly line has a specific skill and is responsible for a specific task. The assembly line manager directs the efforts of each worker so that, together, the workers produce a fully functional car. Similarly, each hardware component, such as the keyboard or printer, and each software package, such as a word processor or electronic spreadsheet, has a specific set of capabilities and a specific function within the computer system. The operating system directs the operations of these components and guarantees that all the components work together.

The most commonly used operating system on microcomputers is DOS. DOS is an abbreviation for Disk Operating System. Disk refers to one of the important hardware resources — hard disks and diskettes — managed by the operating system. DOS actually includes two related types of operating systems: MS-DOS and PC-DOS. IBM microcomputers use PC-DOS (which stands for Personal Computer Disk Operating System). IBM compatibles, or computers produced by other manufacturers, use MS-DOS. MS-DOS stands for Microsoft Disk Operating System. Microsoft is the name of the company that produces MS-DOS.

MS-DOS and PC-DOS manage the hardware and software resources within a computer system in similar ways. Both allow you to interact and use the operating system in the same way. This text uses MS-DOS.

The two most recent releases, or **versions**, of DOS are Versions 5.0 and 6.0. Like other versions that preceded them, these versions improve the performance of DOS, extend its abilities to work with newer types of hardware and software, include additional features, and correct problems found in earlier versions.

Using Files and Filenames

When you work on a computer system, the software you use and the documents you produce are stored in a work space called **RAM**, or Random Access Memory. This memory is *volatile*. If you turn off the power to the computer system, or if the power fails, you lose your working copy of the software and, more importantly, your document. For this reason, you must periodically save your work onto a diskette or hard disk.

When you save your work, your document is stored in a file. A **file** consists of a certain amount of storage space on a diskette or hard disk that is set aside for the contents of your document. You give each file a unique **filename** to identify both its contents and its location on the diskette. This filename can consist of one to eight characters. The characters can include letters of the alphabet or numbers (such as 0 through 9). For example, if you prepare a resume, you could store the document in a file with the filename RESUME. If you produce two different versions of your resume, you can store the first version in a file named RESUME1 and the second in a file named RESUME2. You *cannot* use the same filename for two different files, even if the files contain the same or similar information. If you attempt to use the name of an existing file, you might replace the contents of that file with another document.

You can also use certain types of symbols, such as an underline or dash, as part of a filename. For example, you might save a copy of your most recent tax records under the filename TAX_RECS and TAX-RECS. Because a filename cannot contain any blank spaces, the underscore and dash are commonly used to separate two parts of the same filename. You cannot use other symbols, such as a slash (/) or asterisk (*), as part of a filename because these symbols are used with DOS commands.

If you need a filename that is longer than eight characters, you can include a **file extension** that contains an additional one to three characters. When you use a file extension, you separate the main part of the filename from the file extension with a period. For example, you might use the filename RESUME.LTR for a file that contains a cover letter for your resume.

Using Drive, Directory, and Path Names

In addition to providing a name for a file, you might also need to tell DOS which disk drive to use when it stores a file. DOS uses **drive names** to distinguish the different disk drives in your computer system. The drive names A: and B: are used for the diskette drives. The drive name C: is used for the hard disk drive. If you work on a computer network, you will also have network drives, such as F:, G:, and H:. When you specify a drive name, be sure that you include the colon immediately after the drive letter.

On a hard disk drive, program and document files are stored in separate storage compartments called **directories**. These directories have names similar to filenames. For example, you might have a directory named DOS that contains the program files included with DOS, and another one named RESUMES that stores the different versions of your resume. When saving a file to a hard disk, you must specify the name of the directory. When you indicate the drive name, directory name, and filename for DOS to use when it stores a file, you are identifying the **path name** for that file. For example, Figure 1-1 shows the full path name for a program file that is stored in a directory named DOS on drive C. Note that a backslash (\) separates the drive name from the directory name, and the directory name from the filename. The path name identifies a specific location for your file.

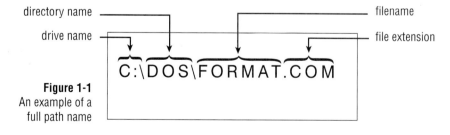

Figure 1-1
An example of a
full path name

How to Follow the Numbered Steps in the DOS Tutorials

Before you start your computer and learn more about DOS, you need to know how to follow the step-by-step instructions in this text. The steps are displayed as numbered items on a shaded background, as shown in Figure 1-2. *Do not attempt to follow these steps.*

To access the Help system:
1. Type **HELP** and press **[Enter]**.
2. Press **[Tab]** and then **[↓]** (Down Arrow) until you highlight <Format>.
3. Press **[Enter]** to display a Help screen on formatting a disk.
4. Press **[PgDn]** to view subsequent Help screens.
5. Press **[Ctrl][Home]** to return to the first Help screen.

Figure 1-2
Example of
step-by-step
instructions

In Figure 1-2 notice that:
- The numbers, letters, and special characters that you type are printed in a distinct bold typeface: Type **HELP**.
- The keys that you press are printed in a distinct bold typeface: Press **[Enter]**.
- Keys that you press in succession are shown as follows: Press **[Tab]** and then **[↓]** (Down Arrow). This indicates that you press the first key and release it, then press the second key and release it.
- Keys that you press simultaneously are shown as follows: Press **[Ctrl][Home]**. This indicates that while pressing the first key, you press the second key, then release both.

As you complete the steps, you can compare screen views on your computer system with those included in the tutorials. Depending on the type of hardware you use, your screen views might be slightly different. Also, unless otherwise noted, the screen views illustrate operations performed with DOS 5.0. If you are using DOS 6.0, you might see messages on the screen that differ slightly from those in DOS 5.0.

Starting a Computer System

To discover how DOS and your computer system work, turn on your computer. The process of powering on a computer system and loading DOS into memory is called **booting** a computer system. The computer system must be able to locate DOS and copy it into memory before you can use the computer system.

When you power on the computer system, you are performing a **cold boot**. During a cold boot, the computer performs a self-test before it loads DOS. If you are using a computer and need to restart the computer for some reason, you can perform a **warm boot** by pressing [Ctrl][Alt][Del] or by pressing the Reset button (if your computer system has this button). The warm boot skips the self-test and the computer reloads DOS into memory.

You must know whether your computer system boots from the hard drive or from a diskette drive. This text assumes you have a hard drive. If this is not the case, your instructor or technical support person will provide you with additional instructions.

To boot your computer system:

1. If drive A contains a diskette, remove the diskette from drive A.

2. Turn the power switch on. You might also need to turn on the monitor. If the computer is already on, ask your instructor or technical support person for permission to turn it off and then back on again. The computer system will perform a self-test and then load DOS into memory from the hard disk drive.

Next, let's perform a warm boot.

3. The easiest way to perform a warm boot with the [Ctrl] [Alt] [Del] keys is to press and hold down **[Ctrl]** and **[Alt]** with your left hand, and press **[Del]** with your right hand. Then, release the three keys. After you press these keys, the screen will clear. DOS will either display the DOS prompt (see Figure 1-3) or, in some cases, will prompt you for the current date and time before it displays the DOS prompt.

DOS prompt ➔

Figure 1-3
DOS prompt after
the system is booted

4. If DOS prompts you for the date, press **[Enter]** to accept the currently set date.

5. If DOS prompts you for the time, press **[Enter]** again to accept the currently set time. DOS then displays the DOS prompt.

If you do not see the DOS prompt on the screen, your computer system might be *customized*, or specifically designed for your needs. If a menu appears with a list of options for using your computer, ask your instructor or technical support person for assistance.

The **DOS prompt** identifies the name of the drive from which the system booted or, in some cases, the drive that DOS automatically uses after the booting process is complete. This drive, called the **default drive** or the **current drive**, is the drive DOS uses until you specify another one.

To the right of the DOS prompt, you will see a small blinking underline called a **cursor**. The cursor identifies your current working position on the screen. If you type a character, that character is displayed on the screen where the cursor was originally positioned. The cursor then appears after the character you typed.

You can enter commands at the DOS prompt to use programs included with DOS. The commands that enable you to work with these programs fall into two groups — internal and external commands. The program instructions for an **internal** command are stored in the computer's memory along with DOS itself. DOS can quickly locate and **execute**, or carry out, those program instructions. The program instructions for an **external** command are stored in a file on a hard disk or diskette. DOS must first locate the program instructions and copy those program instructions into RAM. Then, the computer system can execute the program instructions.

Identifying the Version of DOS

You decide to test the use of some simple DOS commands so that you can understand how to work with DOS. First, you want to use the VER command to find out what version of DOS is installed on your computer system. The VER command is an internal command. DOS obtains the instructions for this command from memory.

To check the DOS version:

1 At the DOS prompt, type **VER**.

2 Press **[Enter]**. DOS displays the version number of DOS that you are using on the computer, and then redisplays the DOS prompt. See Figure 1-4.

Figure 1-4
The VER command displays the version of DOS

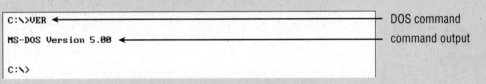

```
C:\>VER  ◄──────────────────────────  DOS command

MS-DOS Version 5.00  ◄─────────────────  command output

C:\>
```

It is important to enter DOS commands exactly as they are written, with the correct punctuation and spacing. However, case does not matter; you can use either uppercase or lowercase.

If you make a typing mistake, you can stop and use the Backspace key to correct the error before you press the Enter key. If DOS displays the message "Bad command or file name," then you mistyped the command. No harm is done. DOS just returns you to the DOS prompt so that you can try again.

When you press the Enter key, DOS executes the instructions for the command you entered at the DOS prompt. If you enter a command and do not press the Enter key, nothing will happen.

Identifying the DOS version is useful for three reasons. First, you can use the VER command to verify that you are using a certain version of DOS on a computer system. Each version of DOS has different capabilities. If you attempt to perform a certain operation with DOS and you experience difficulties, you can check the version of DOS to be sure you are using the one containing this feature.

Second, if you are experiencing difficulties in using a software package on your computer system, you can contact the company that produces that software. One of the first questions a technical support representative might ask you is what version of DOS you are using. The company representative uses that information as a starting point for troubleshooting the problem that you are experiencing with your computer system.

Finally, when you install a new software package on a computer system, the instructions for that new software product might indicate that you need a specific version of DOS. Before you install the software, you should check the DOS version used on that computer system.

Setting the Date and Time

Next, you decide to verify that the date and time are set correctly on your computer system. The correct date and time are important because DOS records the date and time when you save a file. For example, if you have two versions of your resume stored in two different files, you can check the date and time each file was saved to determine which file contains the most recent version of your resume.

You should change the date and time if they are not correct. For example, during the year, you will need to change from standard time to daylight savings time and vice versa. To change the date and time, you use the DATE and TIME commands.

To check and change the current date:

● Type **DATE** and press **[Enter]**. On the next available line, DOS displays the date used on your computer. On the line after the one with the current date, DOS displays a prompt for you to enter a new date. See Figure 1-5. This type of prompt is an example of a request for information from a program.

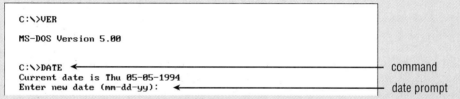

Figure 1-5
The DATE command prompts for a new date

❷ Type the date of your next birthday in the same format shown in parentheses. For example, if your next birthday is October 31, 1994, type **10-31-94** and press **[Enter]**. DOS displays the DOS prompt again.

To verify the new date, you can enter the DATE command again, or you can use [F3] (Repeat) to recall the last DOS command that you entered.

To verify the new date:

● Press **[F3]**. DOS displays the previous DATE command that you entered. See Figure 1-6. If [F3] does not work, then you might have pressed [Enter] twice after the last command you entered. You will then have to type the command again.

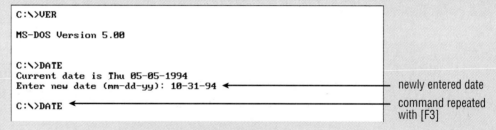

Figure 1-6
The DATE command repeated with the [F3] function key

❷ Press **[Enter]**. DOS displays the date that you previously entered and also automatically determines the day of the week for the new date — your next birthday.

If you were to save a file now, DOS would record your birthday as the date the file was saved. This would be confusing. Let's change the date back to the current date.

❸ Type the current date and press **[Enter]**. DOS displays the DOS prompt again.

If you know in advance what date you want to use, you can type the DATE command followed by the date. For example, if you want to change the date to March 21, 1994, you can enter DATE 3-21-94. DOS will not prompt you for the date and will not show you the date change.

Although [F3] (Repeat) is useful, it allows you to recall only the last DOS command. DOS 5.0 contains a new feature called **DOSKEY** that keeps track of the last 20 or so commands you enter so that you can recall a command. To use this feature, you just enter the command DOSKEY at the DOS prompt. Later, you can recall a command using the [↑] (Up Arrow) and [↓] (Down Arrow) keys.

To activate DOSKEY:

❶ Type **DOSKEY** and press **[Enter]**. In most cases, DOS will display the message "DOSKey installed." If you do not see this message, then DOSKEY is already loaded.

After you enter a few commands, you will use DOSKEY to recall a specific command. Next, you want to check the current time.

To check and change the time on your computer system:

❶ Type **TIME** and press **[Enter]**. DOS displays the current time in hours, minutes, seconds, and either "a" for a.m. or "p" for p.m. See Figure 1-7. On the next line, DOS prompts you to enter a new time.

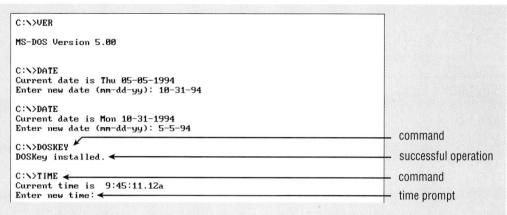

```
C:\>VER

MS-DOS Version 5.00


C:\>DATE
Current date is Thu 05-05-1994
Enter new date (mm-dd-yy): 10-31-94

C:\>DATE
Current date is Mon 10-31-1994
Enter new date (mm-dd-yy): 5-5-94

C:\>DOSKEY
DOSKey installed.

C:\>TIME
Current time is  9:45:11.12a
Enter new time:
```

command ◄

successful operation ◄

command ◄

time prompt ◄

Figure 1-7
The TIME command
displays the current
time and prompts
for a new time

➋ Type a new time that is one hour ahead of the current time and press **[Enter]**. For example, if the time is 10:30 a.m., type 11:30a and press [Enter]. If the time is 3:30 p.m., type 4:30p and press [Enter]. If you do not type "a" or "p," DOS assumes that the time is an a.m. time.

➌ Press **[↑]** (Up Arrow). DOSKEY displays the previous TIME command. You can use DOSKEY to recall previously entered commands at any time while you are working at the DOS prompt.

➍ Press **[Enter]**. DOS displays the current time and prompts for a new time.

If you were to save a file now, DOS would record the incorrect time. Let's change the time back to the current time.

➎ Type the correct time and press **[Enter]**.

As when entering the DATE command, if you know in advance what time you want to use, you can enter the new time with the TIME command. For example, if you enter TIME 5:00p, DOS will make the change and display the DOS prompt again, without asking you for any other information.

Clearing the Screen

You notice that the screen is cluttered with commands, DOS messages and prompts, and your responses to the prompts. Now, you are working at the bottom of the screen. To clear the screen so that you can work more easily, you use the CLS command.

To clear the screen:

➊ Type **CLS** and press **[Enter]**. DOS clears the screen and displays the DOS prompt and cursor in the upper-left corner of the screen.

Clearing the screen before issuing commands is a good habit to develop because it enables you to work more efficiently.

Using On-Line Help

When you acquired your computer, you also bought a word processing software package. Now, you want to use this software to design a new resume. Because you want to store the final file on a diskette, you must next format a diskette, or prepare it for use on your computer system. You need help in locating the correct command and how to use it once you find it.

DOS 5.0 contains a command, HELP, which provides on-line assistance with DOS commands. In DOS 6.0, the HELP command provides more extensive help. Because the command functions differently in these two versions, follow the instructions for the version of DOS that you are using.

Using the DOS 5.0 HELP Command

You want to use the HELP command to locate the correct command to use for preparing a diskette. Then, you want to locate more detailed information on that command.

To locate general help information on DOS commands:

● Type **HELP** and press **[Enter]**. DOS displays a screen of help information, displays the message "More," and then stops. See Figure 1-8. At the top of this screen, DOS 5.0 instructs you to type HELP followed by the name of a command for which you want more detailed information. Notice that this screen contains explanations for the CLS and DATE commands. After examining the list of commands, you are ready to view the next screen.

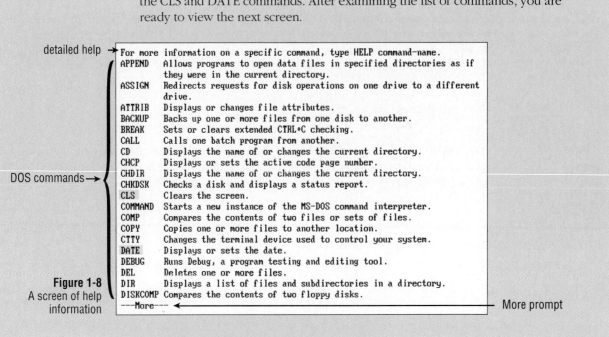

detailed help →

DOS commands →

Figure 1-8
A screen of help
information

```
For more information on a specific command, type HELP command-name.
APPEND    Allows programs to open data files in specified directories as if
          they were in the current directory.
ASSIGN    Redirects requests for disk operations on one drive to a different
          drive.
ATTRIB    Displays or changes file attributes.
BACKUP    Backs up one or more files from one disk to another.
BREAK     Sets or clears extended CTRL+C checking.
CALL      Calls one batch program from another.
CD        Displays the name of or changes the current directory.
CHCP      Displays or sets the active code page number.
CHDIR     Displays the name of or changes the current directory.
CHKDSK    Checks a disk and displays a status report.
CLS       Clears the screen.
COMMAND   Starts a new instance of the MS-DOS command interpreter.
COMP      Compares the contents of two files or sets of files.
COPY      Copies one or more files to another location.
CTTY      Changes the terminal device used to control your system.
DATE      Displays or sets the date.
DEBUG     Runs Debug, a program testing and editing tool.
DEL       Deletes one or more files.
DIR       Displays a list of files and subdirectories in a directory.
DISKCOMP  Compares the contents of two floppy disks.
---More---
```

More prompt

➋ Press **[Space]** or any other key. DOS displays another Help screen on DOS commands. Notice that this screen contains an explanation of the DOSKEY command. After examining the other commands, you find the one you need — the FORMAT command. Before you return to the DOS prompt, you want to examine the remaining screens.

➌ Press **[Space]** or any other key to display the third screen of information. Notice the explanation of the HELP command.

➍ Press **[Space]** or any other key to display the fourth Help screen. This screen contains explanations of the TIME and VER commands. On your computer the VER command might appear in the last Help screen.

➎ Press **[Space]** or any other key to display the last Help screen and the DOS prompt.

Next, you are ready to view more detailed help on the FORMAT command. As pointed out on each of the Help screens, you can type HELP followed by the DOS command for which you want information.

To obtain help information on the FORMAT command:

➊ Type **HELP FORMAT** and press **[Enter]**. Be sure you include a space between the commands HELP and FORMAT. DOS 5.0 displays a Help screen with more specific details on the use of the FORMAT command. See Figure 1-9.

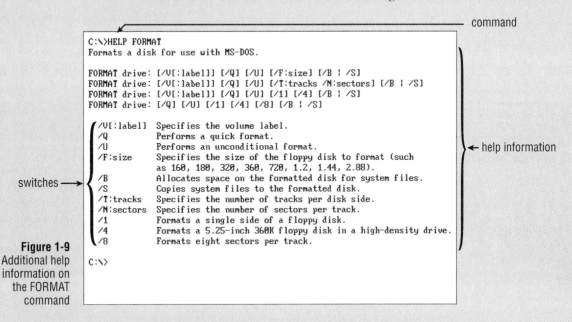

Figure 1-9
Additional help information on the FORMAT command

This Help screen tells you that the FORMAT command formats a diskette for use with DOS. Then, it shows the ways in which you can enter the command. For example, first you type FORMAT. Then, you specify the name of the drive containing the diskette that you want to format. The drive name is a required **parameter**, or item of information, because the command cannot operate without this information. You must also leave a space between the command and the drive name.

Optional parameters, or switches, are listed within square brackets. A **switch** modifies the way in which a command operates. Note that each switch starts with a slash (/) and is followed by one or more additional codes. For example, when you use the **System switch** (/S) with the FORMAT command, DOS formats the diskette and adds the DOS system files to the diskette. The DOS **system files** are the three files that constitute the operating system software. The resulting diskette is called a **system disk** or **boot disk** because you can use it to start the computer system from a diskette drive. If you do not use this switch, DOS still formats the diskette, but it does not add the DOS system files to the diskette.

Before you continue, you decide to print a copy of this Help screen to use later for reference.

To print the Help screen:

① Be sure the printer is operational. If necessary, ask your instructor or technical support person to show you how to use the printer.

② Press **[Print Screen]**. If your keyboard does not have this key, press [Shift][PrtSc].

③ Press the Form Feed (FF) button on the printer to advance the paper in the printer. If nothing happens when you press Form Feed, press the On Line button, press Form Feed again, and then press On Line a final time.

④ Remove your printed copy of the Help screen from the printer.

You can obtain the same type of help information more quickly with the Help switch. The **Help switch** (/?) works with any DOS command. Like the HELP command, the Help switch is a new feature in DOS 5.0.

To use the Help switch with the FORMAT command:

① Type **FORMAT /?** and press **[Enter]**. DOS displays the same Help screen produced by the HELP command. *Be sure you type a slash rather than a backslash.* A slash (/) leans to the right; a backslash (\) leans to the left. If you type a backslash, DOS displays the error message "Too many parameters" and then displays the DOS prompt again.

With on-line Help, you can quickly locate information on the DOS commands that you use and learn more about their capabilities.

If you want to take a break and you are working in a computer lab, ask your instructor or technical support person whether it is necessary to turn off the computer. If so, locate the power switch and turn it to the "OFF" position. Then, locate the power switch for the monitor and turn off the power. If you want to continue, skip to the section entitled "Formatting Diskettes."

Using the DOS 6.0 HELP Command

You want to use the HELP command to locate the correct command to use for preparing a diskette. Then, you want to locate more detailed information on that command.

To access the Help system:

1. Type **HELP** and press **[Enter]**. DOS 6.0 displays a Command Reference with a partial list of DOS commands in alphabetical order. See Figure 1-10.

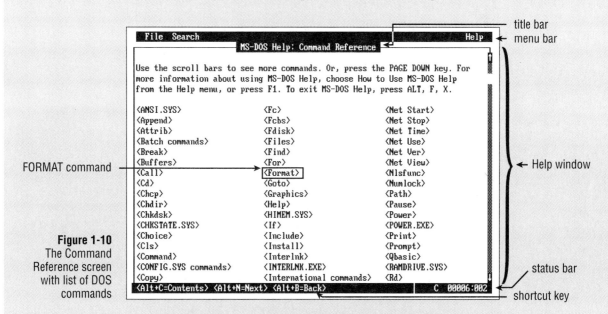

Figure 1-10
The Command Reference screen with list of DOS commands

The menu bar at the top of the screen displays the names of the menus you can use with the DOS 6.0 Help system. The *title bar* identifies the name of the screen that you are using. The *Help window* is the area of the screen where DOS 6.0 displays an index of commands or help information. The *status bar* at the bottom of the screen provides you with a list of *shortcut keys* to navigate around, and use, the Help system. You notice the FORMAT command. This is the command you need to use to prepare the diskette so that it can store files.

If you want to see the remainder of the help information, you can press [PgDn] (Page Down) to view the next screen. To return to the previous screen, you press [PgUp] (Page Up). These two keys are located to the right of the main keyboard.

2. Press **[Tab]** to move the cursor to the beginning of the second column of commands. Then, press **[↓]** (Down Arrow) until you highlight <Format>.

3. Press **[Enter]**. DOS 6.0 displays a Help screen with information on how to format a diskette. See Figure 1-11 on the following page.

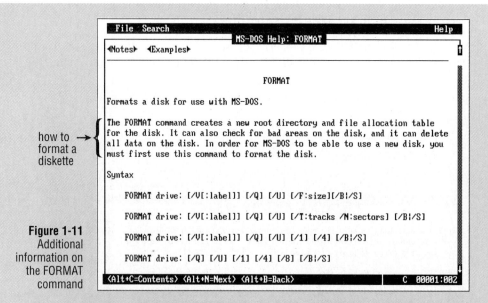

how to → format a diskette

Figure 1-11
Additional information on the FORMAT command

Press **[PgDn]** (Page Down). DOS 6.0 displays another Help screen informing you that the drive name is a required *parameter*, or item of information. The FORMAT command cannot operate without this information. Then, optional parameters, or switches, are explained. Note that each switch starts with a slash (/) and is followed by one or more additional codes. A *switch* modifies the way in which a command operates.

Press **[PgDn]** three more times. DOS 6.0 displays help information on the System switch (/S).

When you use the *System switch* with the FORMAT command, DOS formats the diskette and adds the DOS system files to the diskette. The DOS *system files* are the three files that constitute the operating system software. The resulting diskette is called a *system disk* or *boot disk* because you can use it to start the computer system from a diskette drive. If you do not use this switch, DOS still formats the diskette, but it does not add the DOS system files to the diskette.

Press **[Ctrl] [Home]**. DOS 6.0 returns you to the first Help screen. The cursor is positioned on a *menu bar* that contains a list of menus from which you can choose.

Press **[→]** (Right Arrow) to position the cursor on the **N** in Notes. Then, press **[Enter]** to select this option. DOS 6.0 displays a Help screen with additional notes on the use of the FORMAT command. See Figure 1-12.

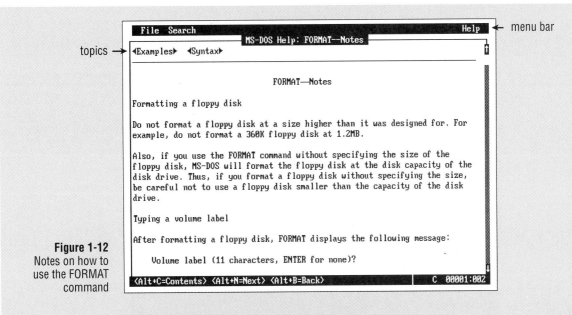

Figure 1-12
Notes on how to
use the FORMAT
command

8 Press **[Enter]** to select the topic Examples. DOS 6.0 illustrates different uses of the FORMAT command. See Figure 1-13.

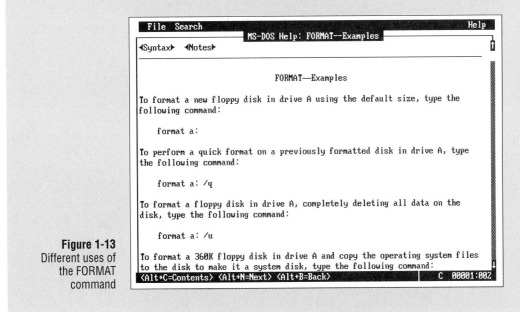

Figure 1-13
Different uses of
the FORMAT
command

Now that you have located the command to format a diskette, you are ready to exit the Help system.

To exit the DOS 6.0 Help system:

🔘 Press **[Alt]**. DOS 6.0 highlights the File menu on the menu bar at the top of the screen. You can select a menu in one of two ways: you can type the character of the menu name that appears in white; or you can use the directional arrow keys to point to the menu that you want to use and then press [Enter].

🔘 Press **[Enter]** to select the File menu. A drop-down menu appears and DOS 6.0 automatically highlights the first command, Print. See Figure 1-14. A *drop-down menu* is a menu that drops down from the menu bar and displays commands for the selected menu.

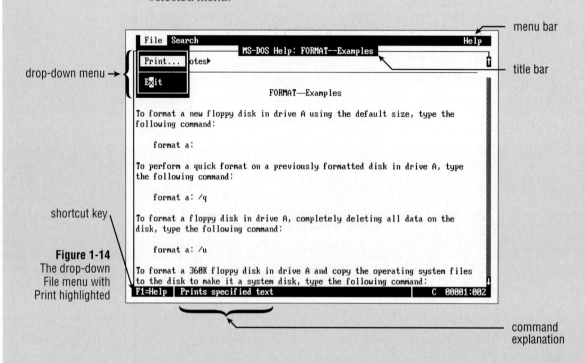

Figure 1-14
The drop-down
File menu with
Print highlighted

🔘 Press **[↓]** to highlight the Exit command. Then, press **[Enter]**. You exit the Help system and return to the DOS prompt.

The DOS 6.0 Help system is quite extensive. If you are in a rush, you can obtain help information with the Help switch. The Help switch (/?) works with any DOS command.

To use the Help switch with the FORMAT command:

🔘 Type **FORMAT /?** and press **[Enter]**. DOS displays a Help screen that summarizes the features of the FORMAT command. See Figure 1-15. *Be sure you type a slash rather than a backslash.* A slash (/) leans to the right; a backslash (\) leans to the left. If you type a backslash, DOS displays the error message "Too many parameters" and then displays the DOS prompt again.

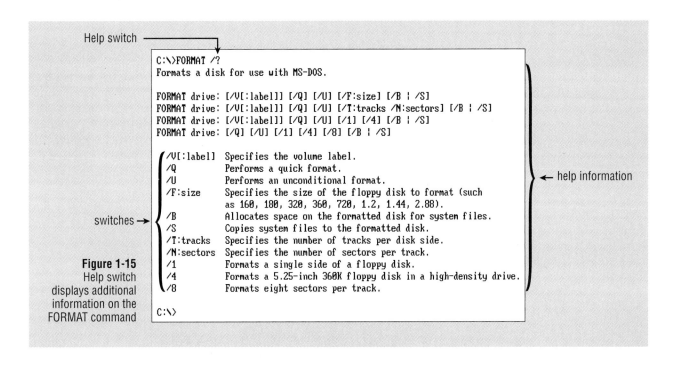

Figure 1-15
Help switch
displays additional
information on the
FORMAT command

Before you continue, you decide to print a copy of this Help screen to use later for reference.

To print the Help screen:

● Be sure the printer is operational. If necessary, ask your instructor or technical support person to show you how to use the printer.

● Press **[Print Screen]**. If your keyboard does not have this key, press [Shift][PrtSc].

● Press the Form Feed (FF) button on the printer to advance the paper in the printer. If nothing happens when you press Form Feed, press the On Line button, press Form Feed again, and then press On Line a final time.

● Remove your printed copy of the Help screen from the printer.

With on-line Help, you can quickly locate information on the DOS commands that you use and learn more about their capabilities.

If you want to take a break and you are working in a computer lab, ask your instructor or technical support person whether it is necessary to turn off the computer. If so, locate the power switch and turn it to the "OFF" position. Then, locate the power switch for the monitor and turn off the power. Otherwise, continue with the next section.

Formatting Diskettes

Now that you have the information you need on the FORMAT command, you are ready to format a diskette. As you can see from your printed copy of the help information on this command, FORMAT prepares a blank, or unformatted, diskette so that DOS can store files on it. During the formatting process, DOS magnetically labels the concentric recording bands, or **tracks**, on the diskette. DOS then subdivides the tracks into sectors. A **sector** is the minimum storage space on a diskette. Each sector can store 512 bytes of data. A **byte** is the storage space used by one character. Figure 1-16 shows the organization of tracks and sectors on a newly formatted diskette.

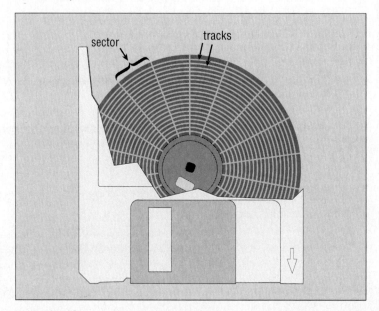

Figure 1-16
Tracks and sectors
on a formatted
3½-inch diskette

Diskettes are sold in two common storage capacities that are referred to as double-density and high-density. A **high-density** diskette stores two to four times as much information as a **double-density** diskette. Each diskette's storage capacity is rated in kilobytes (K or KB) or megabytes (M or MB). A **kilobyte** is 1024 bytes and a **megabyte** is 1024 kilobytes.

Because diskettes are available in two sizes and two storage capacities, you want to be sure that you purchase the proper type for use in your computer (Figure 1-17). The difference in storage capacities depends on the number of tracks and sectors formatted on each side of a diskette.

Size	Density	Storage Capacity	Number of Sides	Number of Tracks	Number of Sectors	Bytes per Sector
5¼"	Double	360K	2	40	9	512
5¼"	High	1.2MB	2	80	15	512
3½"	Double	720K	2	80	9	512
3½"	High	1.44MB	2	80	18	512

Figure 1-17
Characteristics of
different types of
diskettes

In some cases, you might need to format a double-density diskette in a high-density disk drive. If this is the case, you can use the **Format Capacity switch**, (/F), with the FORMAT command to ensure that the diskette is formatted to the proper storage capacity. Otherwise, DOS might report a large number of defective sectors as it tries to format the double-density diskette as a high-density diskette.

You can also reformat a diskette that already contains information. If you do, you will erase all the information on the diskette. Before you format a diskette, be sure it does not contain any important information that you need.

The FORMAT command is an external command, so DOS must locate the program instructions for this command in a file on disk and then load the program into memory before using it.

This book includes a 3½-inch double-density Data Disk with files. You need two additional copies so that you can use one diskette for the DOS Tutorials and one for the DOS Exercises. Before you can produce these copies, you must first format two diskettes.

After you find out whether your computer system has a double-density or a high-density disk drive, follow the instructions appropriate to your computer.

To format a double-density diskette in a *double-density drive*:

1. Insert an unformatted, or blank, double-density diskette into a disk drive and, if necessary, close the drive door. See Figure 1-18, which illustrates how to insert a 3½-inch diskette or a 5¼-inch diskette into a corresponding disk drive. Make sure the blank diskette matches the size of the disk drive.

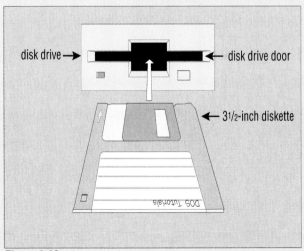
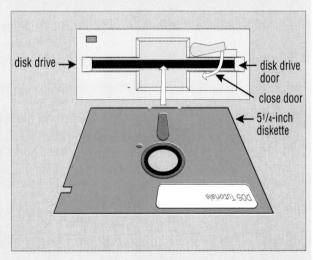

Figure 1-18
Inserting a 3½-inch and a 5¼-inch diskette into a disk drive

2. If your diskette is in drive A, type **FORMAT A:** and press **[Enter]**. If your diskette is in drive B, type **FORMAT B:** and press **[Enter]**. See Figure 1-19 on the following page.

DOS then prompts you to insert a new diskette into drive A, or drive B. If you have not inserted the diskette yet, do so now.

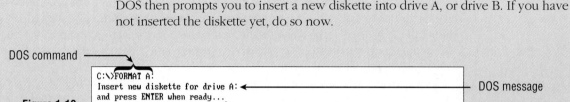

DOS command

Figure 1-19
Formatting a
double-density
diskette in a
double-density drive

DOS message

prompt to press
[Enter]

③ After you insert the diskette, press **[Enter]**. You will know DOS is formatting the diskette when you see the first message, "Checking disk format." The second DOS message tells you that DOS is verifying the storage capacity of the diskette. Then, DOS displays a percent to show you how much of the formatting process is complete. When it reaches 100%, DOS informs you that the formatting process is complete. If DOS displays an error message at any time, try another diskette or ask your instructor or technical support person for assistance.

As noted earlier, if your computer system has a high-density disk drive, you need to use the Format Capacity switch to format a double-density diskette in the drive. Because a 3½-inch double-density diskette can store 720K, you must specify 720 for the capacity. If you are using a 5¼-inch diskette, you must specify 360 for the capacity.

To format a double-density diskette in a *high-density drive*:

① Insert an unformatted, or blank, double-density diskette into a disk drive and, if necessary, close the drive door. See Figure 1-18.

② If your diskette is in drive A, type **FORMAT A: /F:720** and press **[Enter]**. If your diskette is in drive B, type **FORMAT B: /F:720** and press **[Enter]**. See Figure 1-20. DOS prompts you to insert a new diskette into drive A, or drive B. If you have not inserted the diskette yet, do so now. The Format Capacity switch, /F:size, tells DOS to format the diskette to a specific storage capacity. Note that DOS uses the word size to indicate capacity.

DOS command
including Format
Capacity switch

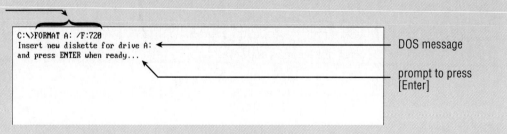

Figure 1-20
Formatting a
double-density
diskette in a
high-density drive

DOS message

prompt to press
[Enter]

③ After you insert the diskette, press **[Enter]**. You will know DOS is formatting the diskette when you see the first message, "Checking disk format." The second DOS message tells you that DOS is verifying the storage capacity of the diskette. Then, DOS displays a percent to show you how much of the formatting process is complete. When it reaches 100%, DOS informs you that the formatting process is complete. If DOS displays an error message at any time, try another diskette or ask your instructor or technical support person for assistance.

While the diskette is formatting, it spins in the disk drive unit and the drive light is on. You should *not* remove a diskette from, or insert a diskette into, a disk drive when the drive light is on. Wait until the drive light is off to safely remove or insert a diskette.

DOS then prompts for a volume label (Figure 1-21). A **volume label** is a name for the diskette that identifies the type of information you store on the diskette. For example, if you intend to store copies of your resumes and cover letters on a diskette, you could name the diskette JOB SEARCH. The volume label, or name, can consist of one to 11 characters and can include spaces. Certain types of symbols, such as a period, are not allowed. If you attempt to use an invalid character, DOS will inform you of this problem and will prompt you again for the volume label.

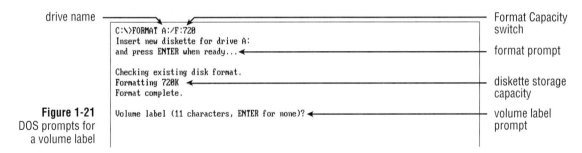

drive name — Format Capacity switch

```
C:\>FORMAT A:/F:720
Insert new diskette for drive A:
and press ENTER when ready...◄─────────────  format prompt

Checking existing disk format.
Formatting 720K  ◄─────────────  diskette storage
Format complete.                 capacity

Volume label (11 characters, ENTER for none)?◄───  volume label
                                                   prompt
```

Figure 1-21
DOS prompts for a volume label

You need to choose a volume label that will be appropriate for both diskettes. Both diskettes will be working copies of your Data Disk, initially containing the same business records, but you will use one diskette for the tutorials and one diskette for the exercises. Let's choose BUSINESS as the volume label.

To enter a volume label for the diskette:

① Type **BUSINESS** and press **[Enter]**. DOS assigns the volume label to the diskette, displays information on how it formatted the diskette, and asks if you want to format another diskette. See Figure 1-22 on the following page.

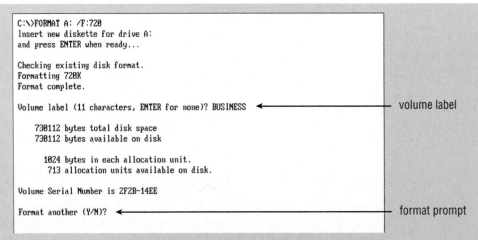

```
C:\>FORMAT A: /F:720
Insert new diskette for drive A:
and press ENTER when ready...

Checking existing disk format.
Formatting 720K
Format complete.

Volume label (11 characters, ENTER for none)? BUSINESS          ◄──────  volume label

    730112 bytes total disk space
    730112 bytes available on disk

    1024 bytes in each allocation unit.
     713 allocation units available on disk.

Volume Serial Number is 2F2B-14EE

Format another (Y/N)?  ◄──────────────────────────────────────────────  format prompt
```

Figure 1-22
DOS assigns a volume label to the diskette and asks if you want to format another diskette

② Because you need two formatted diskettes for Tutorial 2, type **Y** for Yes and press **[Enter]**. DOS prompts you to insert a new diskette into the drive. *If you already have two blank, formatted diskettes with the volume label BUSINESS, skip to Step 5.*

③ Insert another unformatted, double-density diskette, and press **[Enter]**. DOS repeats the formatting process.

④ When DOS prompts you for the volume label for this diskette, type **BUSINESS** and press **[Enter]**. You want to use the same volume label since you will use these diskettes later to make two working copies of the Data Disk that accompanies this text.

⑤ When DOS asks if you want to format another diskette, type **N** for No and press **[Enter]**. Then, DOS returns you to the DOS prompt. See Figure 1-23.

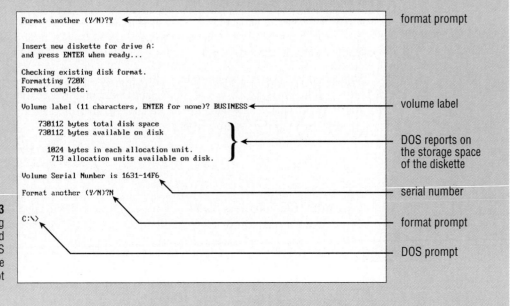

```
Format another (Y/N)?Y  ◄─────────────────────────────────────────────  format prompt


Insert new diskette for drive A:
and press ENTER when ready...

Checking existing disk format.
Formatting 720K
Format complete.

Volume label (11 characters, ENTER for none)? BUSINESS ◄───────────────  volume label

    730112 bytes total disk space
    730112 bytes available on disk        ⎫
                                          ⎬ ◄───  DOS reports on
    1024 bytes in each allocation unit.   ⎭       the storage space
     713 allocation units available on disk.      of the diskette

Volume Serial Number is 1631-14F6

Format another (Y/N)?N  ◄─────────────────────────────────────────────  serial number

                                                                          format prompt
C:\>  ◄───────────────────────────────────────────────────────────────  DOS prompt
```

Figure 1-23
After formatting the second diskette, DOS returns to the DOS prompt

After formatting a diskette, DOS displays information on the storage capacity of the newly formatted diskette. The first number shows the total amount of storage space on the diskette in bytes. The second number shows how much of this storage space is available for use, again in bytes. Usually, these two numbers match and indicate that you can use all of the storage space available on the diskette. If these numbers don't match, you might see a message indicating that there are a certain number of bytes in bad sectors. When DOS formats a diskette, it also checks the surface of the diskette for defects. **Bad sectors** are defective areas on the diskette that DOS marks as unusable. You can still use the rest of the diskette. When DOS records information onto the diskette later, it does not use sectors marked as defective or bad.

On the next line, DOS reports on the size of each allocation unit and the total number of allocation units on the diskette. An **allocation unit** is the minimum storage space that DOS uses when it records the contents of a file on the diskette. On high-density diskettes, an allocation unit is the same size as a sector. This means that DOS stores information on a high-density diskette one sector at a time. On double-density diskettes, an allocation unit consists of two sectors. This means that DOS uses a minimum of two sectors when it stores information on a double-density diskette — even if DOS needs less than two sectors of diskette storage space for the file.

After DOS reports on how the storage space on the diskette is allocated, it identifies the serial number assigned to the diskette. The **serial number** is a unique ID number produced by DOS from the date and time on the computer system. The serial number provides another way to identify a diskette. (Your serial number will be different from the one shown in Figure 1-23.) Finally, DOS asks if you want to format another diskette.

If DOS reports more than a few thousand bytes of bad sectors, the diskette itself could be defective. If you format another diskette and DOS does not report any bad sectors for that diskette, the first diskette that you formatted was probably defective and should be thrown out. If you use a diskette with a large number of bad sectors, the condition might become worse and you could lose important information stored on the diskette.

After you format a diskette, you should place a label on the diskette to identify its contents. You can use the blank adhesive label provided with the diskette when you purchased it. Before you place labels on the newly formatted diskettes, write a short description on each label to identify the contents. The description does not have to be the same as the volume label. You want to label each diskette so that you can identify which diskette to use for the tutorials and which to use for the exercises. On one label, write DOS Tutorials and, on the other label, write DOS Exercises. Figure 1-24 on the following page shows how to place a label on a 3½-inch and a 5¼-inch diskette. If you have already placed the blank label on the diskette, use a felt-tip pen to gently write the description on the label. Do *not* use a ballpoint pen, ink pen, or pencil to write on the label. You might damage the surface of the diskette.

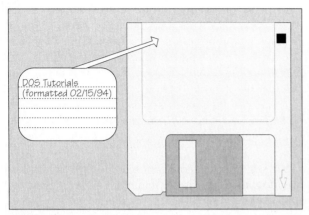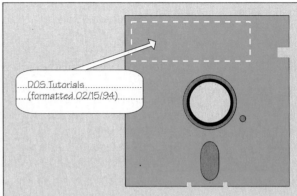

Figure 1-24
Applying an adhesive label to a 3¹/₂-inch and a 5¹/₄-inch diskette

Changing the Default Drive

Now that you have formatted diskettes, you are ready to make duplicate copies of the Data Disk that came with this book. You decide to change drives so that you can make the copy from drive A (or drive B). To change from one drive to another at the DOS prompt, you type the name of the drive. You must include the colon (:) after the letter of the alphabet that identifies the drive. Otherwise, DOS assumes that you have entered a command. It will then look for the program instructions and inform you that you entered a "Bad command or file name" when it cannot find the program instructions. Also, do not confuse the semicolon (;) with the colon (:).

To change to the drive with the Data Disk:

❶ Remove the newly formatted diskette from the disk drive that you are using, and insert the Data Disk.

❷ If the Data Disk is in drive A, type **A:** and press **[Enter]**. If the Data Disk is in drive B, type **B:** and press **[Enter]**. DOS updates the DOS prompt to show the new default drive. See Figure 1-25.

Figure 1-25
Changing the
default drive
from C to A

```
C:\>A:                                           drive name

A:\>                                             previous default
                                                 drive
                                                 current default drive
```

Making a Copy of a Diskette

Now, you are ready to copy the Data Disk. It is important to copy diskettes that contain critical information, such as documents you create and software you use. You can keep the extra copies of diskettes in reserve as **backup** copies. That way, if the original diskette or working copy fails, you should immediately make a duplicate of your backup copy. Then, you use one of the two diskettes as your working copy.

The DISKCOPY command makes a copy of a diskette. When you use this command, you might need to specify the names of the drives that contain the source diskette and a target diskette:

DISKCOPY *source target*

The **source diskette** is the diskette you want to copy. The **target diskette** is the diskette that you copy to (Figure 1-26).

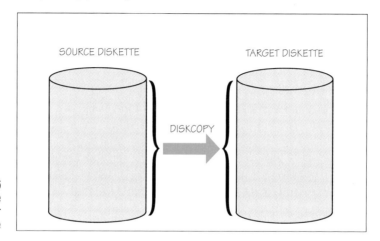

Figure 1-26
Copying an entire
diskette to another
diskette

You often use the same drive for both the source and target diskettes. This command requires you to use diskettes of the same size and same capacity. You cannot perform a disk copy from a double-density diskette to a high-density diskette, or vice versa. Also, you cannot use this command to make a backup copy of your hard disk drive. It works only with diskettes.

If you perform a disk copy from drive A (or drive B) and do not specify the source drive and target drive, DOS assumes you want to use the default drive.

You want two copies of the Data Disk provided with this book. Because the Data Disk is a double-density diskette, you must use another double-density diskette for the target diskette. However, you can perform the disk copy in either a double-density or high-density disk drive.

Before you make copies of the Data Disk, you should **write-protect** the diskette so that the computer cannot record anything onto the diskette. That way, the files are protected from accidental deletion.

To write-protect a 3½-inch diskette, hold the diskette so that the label on the diskette faces away from you with the metal shutter on bottom. On the upper-left side of the diskette, you will see a rectangular notch in the diskette with a square plastic tab in that notch. With your fingernail, press on the square tab until it slides up and exposes an open square hole in the diskette (Figure 1-27 on the following page). The diskette is now write-protected.

if open, the disk is
locked; if blocked,
the disk is unlocked

move plastic
tab up to lock the disk

metal shutter

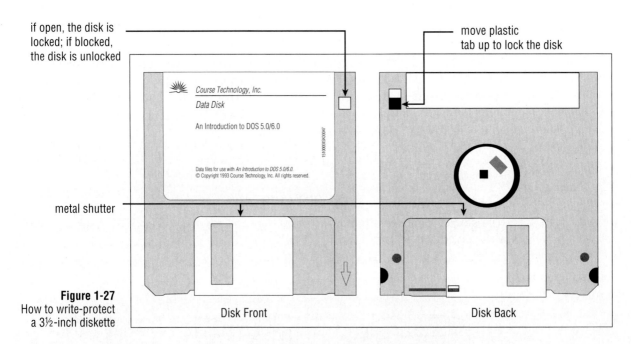

Figure 1-27
How to write-protect
a 3½-inch diskette

Disk Front

Disk Back

Now you are ready to make two copies of the Data Disk.

To copy the Data Disk:

1. Be sure the current drive is the one with the Data Disk.

2. Type **DISKCOPY** and press **[Enter]**. DOS prompts you to insert the source diskette, the diskette that you want to copy. The source diskette — the Data Disk — is already in the disk drive. *Because you did not specify a source drive and a target drive, DOS assumes that this disk drive will be used for both the source diskette and the target diskette.*

3. Press **[Space]** or any other key to continue. The DISKCOPY program copies part of the diskette into memory. It also identifies the diskette specifications including the number of tracks, the number of sectors per track, and the number of sides formatted on this diskette. Then it stops and prompts you to insert the target diskette. See Figure 1-28.

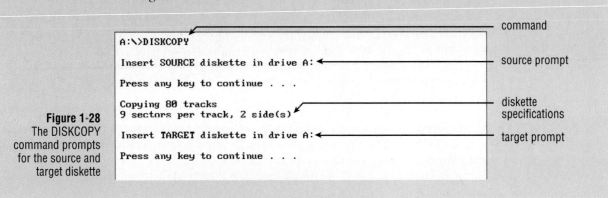

command

```
A:\>DISKCOPY

Insert SOURCE diskette in drive A:

Press any key to continue . . .

Copying 80 tracks
9 sectors per track, 2 side(s)

Insert TARGET diskette in drive A:

Press any key to continue . . .
```

source prompt

diskette
specifications

target prompt

Figure 1-28
The DISKCOPY
command prompts
for the source and
target diskette

④ When you are prompted for the target diskette, remove the Data Disk from the drive after the drive light is off, insert the DOS Tutorials diskette and press **[Space]** or any other key. The DISKCOPY program copies part of the contents of the first diskette from memory onto this new diskette. Then it stops and prompts you to insert the source diskette again. The DISKCOPY program is now ready to copy another part of the Data Disk.

⑤ When prompted to insert the source diskette, remove the target diskette from the disk drive after the drive light is off, insert the Data Disk, and press **[Space]** or any other key. The DISKCOPY program copies another part of the Data Disk into memory. Then it stops and prompts you to insert the target diskette again.

⑥ When prompted to insert the target diskette, remove the Data Disk from the drive after the drive light is off, insert the DOS Tutorials diskette, and press **[Space]** or any other key. The DISKCOPY program copies the remainder of the contents of the Data Disk from memory onto the target diskette. Then it asks if you want to copy another diskette.

⑦ Remove the newly prepared disk copy.

⑧ Insert the original source diskette (the Data Disk), type **Y** for Yes and press **[Enter]**. The DISKCOPY command will repeat the same process. However, this time your target diskette is the DOS Exercises diskette. After you make both copies of the Data Disk, type **N** for No. DOS displays the DOS prompt.

The duplicate copies are exact copies of the original Data Disk, except for one feature. Each diskette has a new serial number. Be sure you have labeled the diskettes so you know which one to use for the tutorials and which to use for the exercises.

Finishing Your Work Session

After you finish using a computer, you should remove any diskettes from the disk drives. You might also need to shut off the power to the computer system.

To end your work session:

① Be sure the DOS prompt is displayed on the screen.

② Be sure the drive light is off. Then, remove the diskette from the disk drive. If you experience any difficulty, ask your instructor or technical support person to show you how to remove the diskette.

③ If you are working in a computer lab, ask your instructor or technical support person whether it is necessary to turn off the computer. If so, locate the power switch and turn it to the "OFF" position. Then, locate the power switch for the monitor and turn off the power to the monitor.

Summary

In this tutorial, you learned that operating system software plays an important role in the management and use of a computer system. DOS is the operating system software used on IBM compatibles and IBM microcomputers. DOS 5.0 and 6.0 are the two most recent versions of DOS.

The primary storage medium used on microcomputer systems is the hard disk and diskette. Diskettes differ in their storage capacities and sizes and must be used in disk drive units that support them. Documents and programs are stored in files on a diskette or on a hard disk. Each file has a filename that you provide. The filename identifies the contents of the file and its location on the disk. You might also need to provide a drive name so that the document is stored on the correct drive.

After you boot a computer system, DOS displays the DOS prompt unless your computer system is customized. You can enter internal or external commands at the DOS prompt. In this tutorial, you used the VER command to display the version of DOS installed on your computer system. You also used the DATE and TIME commands to set, or verify, the date and time used by the computer system. You cleared the screen with the CLS command.

The FORMAT command formats a diskette so that you can use the diskette in the computer system. The Format Capacity switch allows you to format double-density diskettes in high-density disk drives.

Both DOS 5.0 and DOS 6.0 contain help features that assist you with locating and using DOS commands. The Help switch in both versions displays a Help screen with information on a command. The HELP command in DOS 5.0 displays a quick reference guide to all the DOS commands. In DOS 6.0, this same command accesses an extensive On-Line Help system with information on the use of the commands, as well as notes and examples.

Command Reference	
CLS	An internal command that clears the screen and displays the DOS prompt and cursor in the upper-left corner of the screen
DATE	An internal command that displays the date used on the computer system, prompts for a new date, and keeps or changes the date
DATE [mm-dd-yy]	An internal command that sets the date on the computer; for example, DATE 5-21-94 sets the date to May 21, 1994
DISKCOPY [source] [target]	An external command that makes a copy of a diskette
[DOS Command] /?	Displays a screen with help information on the specified DOS command; for example, DATE /? displays help information on the DATE command
DOSKEY	An external command that keeps track of commands entered at the DOS prompt and that allows you to recall the commands with [↑] and [↓]
FORMAT [drive name]	An external command that prepares a diskette for use on a computer system by formatting the diskette to the highest storage capacity of the disk drive; for example, FORMAT A: formats the diskette in drive A
FORMAT [drive name] /F:<size>	An external command that prepares a diskette for use on a computer system by formatting the diskette to the specified storage capacity; for example, FORMAT A: /F:720 formats a 3½-inch double-density diskette to 720K
HELP	DOS 5.0: An external command that displays an alphabetical list of DOS commands with a brief explanation of each command, one screen at a time

DOS 6.0: An external command that accesses the DOS 6.0 Help system and displays an alphabetical list of DOS commands for which help information is available |

HELP [DOS Command]	DOS 5.0: An external command that displays a Help screen with help information on the specified DOS command
	DOS 6.0: An external command that accesses the DOS 6.0 Help system and displays a Help screen with help information on the specified DOS command
	For example, in DOS 5.0 and 6.0, HELP DATE displays help information on the DATE command
TIME	An internal command that displays the time used on a computer system, prompts for a new time, and keeps or changes the time
TIME [hh:mm:ss]	An internal command that sets the time on a computer system to a specific time; for example, TIME 10:30a sets the time to 10:30 a.m.
VER	An internal command that displays the version of DOS used on a computer system

Questions

1. Identify two important types of operations performed by operating system software.   *manages resources   input output*

2. What feature do diskettes and hard disks have in common?   *drive names*

3. What are the two common storage capacities for double-density and high-density diskettes?

4. What is a filename and why is it important?

5. What is a drive name and why is it important?

6. What information does the DOS prompt provide?

7. What is the default drive?

8. Name one reason for identifying the version of DOS that you use on your computer system. How do you find out what the version is?

9. If you make a typing mistake as you enter a DOS command, how can you correct that mistake?

10. Why is it necessary to press the Enter key after you type a command?

11. If DOS displays the message "Bad command or file name" when you enter a command, what is the likely cause of the error?

12. What key can you use at the DOS prompt to repeat the last DOS command that you entered?

13. How would you change the date on a computer system from March 20, 1994 to March 21, 1994?

14. When you check the time on your computer system, you find that the time is set at 7:15 a.m., but the time is actually 7:25 p.m. What command can you enter to correct this setting and how would you enter it?

15. What is a switch? How are switches used? Give one example of a switch.
    modifies the way command operates

16. What is the Help switch and how do you use it?

17. What command can you use to obtain help information on a DOS command? How does that command work in the version of DOS that you use?

18. What does DOS do when it formats a diskette? What is a track? What is a sector?

19. What is an allocation unit?

20. Double-density and high-density diskettes differ in storage capacity and in size. What feature(s) account for the different storage capacities of these diskettes?

21. What must you specify when you use the FORMAT command to format a diskette?

22. What command would you use to format a double-density diskette with a storage capacity of 720K in a high-density disk drive with a storage capacity of 1.44M?

23. What command would you use to format a double-density diskette with a storage capacity of 360K in a high-density disk drive with a storage capacity of 1.2M?

24. What happens if you format a double-density diskette in a high-density drive and do not specify the storage capacity of the double-density diskette?

25. What is a volume label?

26. How do you change the default drive?

27. What command can you use to make a copy of a diskette? How does it work?

28. What command would you enter to perform a disk copy if the DOS prompt is C:\ and the source and target diskettes will be in drive A?

29. When you perform a disk copy, what two features must the diskettes have in common?

30. What does DOSKEY do, and how do you use it?

31. What command would you use to format a DD disk in HD drive?

Tutorial Assignments

1. **Issuing DOS Commands**: After you boot your computer system and access the DOS prompt, use DOS commands to answer the following questions. List the full command that you use for each step.
   a. What version of DOS is installed on the computer system?
   b. Are the date and time settings correct? If not, how did you correct them?
   c. What happens when you clear the screen?
   d. After DOS executes a command, does DOS always return to the same drive? How can you tell? What does this feature tell you about DOS?

2. **Setting the Time**: Assume that the time on your computer system is incorrect. Adjust the time in each of the following steps and answer the questions.
   a. Check the current setting for the time. What command did you enter? What time is your computer system using?
   b. If the time is an a.m. time, change it to a p.m. time. If the time is a p.m. time, change it to an a.m. time. What command did you enter? Did DOS change the time? How did you verify it?
   c. Change the time to 7:30 without specifying an a.m. or p.m. time. What command did you enter? Check the time. Is DOS using an a.m. or a p.m. time? What does this feature tell you about DOS?
   d. Assume the time should be 7:30 p.m. What command would you enter to set the time?
   e. Set the time back to the correct time.

3. **Accessing On-Line Help**: From the DOS prompt, obtain help information on the TIME command with the Help switch and then with the HELP command. As you perform these operations, answer the following questions.
   a. What command did you enter when you used the Help switch?
   b. How did you enter the HELP command?
   c. From the type of information that the HELP command displays, you should know whether your computer system uses DOS 5.0 or DOS 6.0. What version does your computer use?
   d. What did you learn about this command from examining the information on the Help screens?

4. **Formatting Diskettes**: Format a new diskette using drive A, or drive B. As you format the diskette, answer the following questions. *You should use a new diskette for this exercise*.
   a. When DOS starts to format the diskette, what storage capacity does it use for the diskette?
   b. After the diskette is formatted, how many total bytes are available? Are there any bad sectors? What is the size of an allocation unit on the diskette?
   c. You should be able to tell from the size of the allocation unit whether you are using a double-density or a high-density diskette. Which type of diskette are you using?
   d. Did you assign a volume label to the diskette? If so, what volume label did you use?

5. **Copying a Diskette**: Use the DISKCOPY command to make a copy of your Data Disk from drive A. You can use the DOS Exercises diskette as the source diskette and the diskette from Tutorial Assignment #4 as the target diskette. As you do, answer the following questions:
   a. The DOS Exercises diskette is a double-density diskette. What type of diskette must you use to perform the disk copy?
   b. What command did you enter to perform a disk copy from drive A or B?
   c. Are you performing the disk copy in a double-density or a high-density drive?
   d. Does the DISKCOPY command warn you that it is replacing the contents of the target diskette?

Tutorial 2

Working with Files

You have decided to start a small business with a friend. The company, Professional Plus, will prepare high-quality resumes, cover letters, and other personal and professional documents for clients. Your business partner has prepared a diskette with files for anticipating startup costs, projecting income, preparing check lists for equipment and insurance, and producing resumes and other documents in different formats.

You know that you and your partner have a lot of work ahead of you. Before you can take on your first client, you will check the contents of the diskette and make sure it contains all the necessary files. Then, in order to build your client base, you will write an advertisement for the local newspaper. Finally, you will print out the business plan, update the various resume templates, and modify other important files to ensure the smooth running and positive image of Professional Plus.

OBJECTIVES

In this tutorial you will learn to:

- Display a list of files stored on a diskette

- Use switches with directory listings

- Use the mouse

- Explore the MS-DOS Editor's Survival Guide

- Create a file with the MS-DOS Editor

- Save a file created with the MS-DOS Editor

- Open an existing file

- View the contents of a text file

- Access the DOS Shell

- Print a text file at the DOS prompt and from the DOS Shell

- Use wildcards to select files

- Copy a file at the DOS prompt and from the DOS Shell

- Rename a file at the DOS prompt and from the DOS Shell

- Delete a file at the DOS prompt and from the DOS Shell

Displaying a Directory

You want to check the contents of the diskette so that you are familiar with the files and their contents. You can use the DIR command. The DIR command displays a list, or **directory**, of the files stored on a diskette or a hard disk. When you use the DIR command, you have to specify the name of the disk drive if it is different from the one you are using. You can use the DIR command to examine your DOS Tutorials diskette, which contains the business files for Professional Plus. If you have not created two working copies of the Data Disk, refer to Tutorial 1, page DOS 27 for instructions.

Before you begin working with DOS, it is a good idea to install DOSKEY. You might remember from Tutorial 1 that DOSKEY allows you to recall previous commands you have entered simply by pressing [↑] and [↓]. Instead of typing a command each time, you can use the arrow keys to find the previously entered command you need.

To activate DOSKEY:

❶ Power on your computer system, and be sure you see the C:\> prompt displayed on the screen. If you see a prompt for some other drive, type **C:** and press **[Enter]** to change to drive C.

❷ Type **DOSKEY** and press **[Enter]**. DOS should display the message "DOSKey installed." If you do not see this message, DOSKEY is already loaded.

Now you are ready to view a directory.

To display a directory of filenames on your DOS Tutorials diskette:

❶ Insert the DOS Tutorials diskette into drive A or drive B.

❷ Type **DIR**, press **[Space]**, type the name of the drive (**A:** or **B:**), and press **[Enter]**. Be sure you leave a space between the DIR command and the drive name. Also, remember to type the colon (:) after the drive letter. DOS displays a partial directory of your diskette. See Figure 2-1.

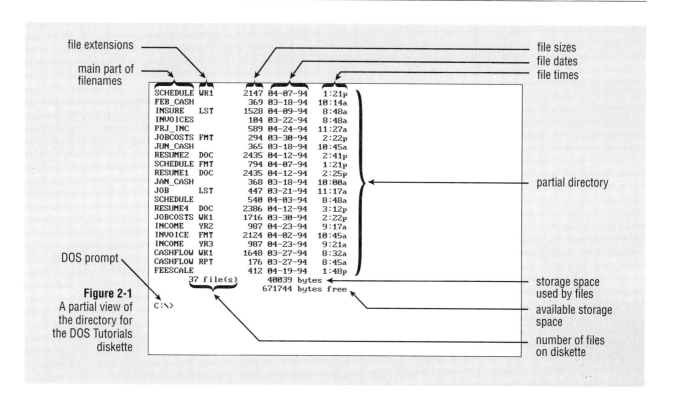

file extensions — main part of filenames — file sizes — file dates — file times — partial directory

DOS prompt

Figure 2-1
A partial view of the directory for the DOS Tutorials diskette

```
SCHEDULE WK1     2147 04-07-94    1:21p
FEB_CASH          369 03-18-94   10:14a
INSURE   LST     1528 04-09-94    8:48a
INVOICES          104 03-22-94    8:48a
PRJ_INC           589 04-24-94   11:27a
JOBCOSTS FMT      294 03-30-94    2:22p
JUN_CASH          365 03-18-94   10:45a
RESUME2  DOC     2435 04-12-94    2:41p
SCHEDULE FMT      794 04-07-94    1:21p
RESUME1  DOC     2435 04-12-94    2:25p
JAN_CASH          368 03-18-94   10:00a
JOB      LST      447 03-21-94   11:17a
SCHEDULE          540 04-03-94    8:48a
RESUME4  DOC     2386 04-12-94    3:12p
JOBCOSTS WK1     1716 03-30-94    2:22p
INCOME   YR2      987 04-23-94    9:17a
INVOICE  FMT     2124 04-02-94   10:45a
INCOME   YR3      987 04-23-94    9:21a
CASHFLOW WK1     1648 03-27-94    8:32a
CASHFLOW RPT      176 03-27-94    8:45a
FEESCALE          412 04-19-94    1:48p
       37 file(s)       40039 bytes
                       671744 bytes free
C:\>
```

storage space used by files — available storage space — number of files on diskette

There are too many files to fit on one screen so the first few files scroll off the screen. If you watch closely, you will see DOS adjust the screen view so that it can display information on all the files. This process of adjusting the screen view is called **scrolling**. The files are listed in **disk order** — the order in which DOS keeps track of the files on the diskette.

The directory contains five columns of information:

- The first column shows the main part of the filename. As you learned in Tutorial 1, a filename can have two parts — the main part of the filename and an optional file extension. The main part consists of one to eight characters. For example, the last file is named FEESCALE.

- The second column shows the file extension for those files that have one. The file extension consists of one to three additional characters. The last file, FEESCALE, does not have a file extension. The file listed before it, CASHFLOW.RPT, has the file extension RPT, an abbreviation for "report." Because the main part of the filename and the file extension are listed in two separate columns, you do not see the period that separates the two parts of the filename.

- The third column lists the size of each file in bytes. FEESCALE is 412 bytes in size.

- The fourth column shows the date that each file was either created or last modified. FEESCALE was created, or last saved, on 4-19-94. Each time you save a file to disk, DOS records the current date with the filename.

- The fifth column shows the time that each file was created or last modified. FEESCALE was created, or last saved, at 1:48 p.m. DOS also updates the file time when you save a file to disk.

Below the directory listing, the DIR command shows the total number of files and the total space used by those files. Your diskette has a total of 37 files that use 40,039 bytes of space. A total of 671,744 bytes of space remain on the diskette. If your diskette has bad sectors, the total space left on your diskette will be different.

Because you were unable to see the first part of this directory listing, you decide to try the Pause and Wide switches with the DIR command. As you recall, a switch modifies how a DOS command operates. The **Pause switch** (/P) modifies the DIR command so that it displays a directory listing one screen at a time. The **Wide switch** (/W) displays filenames in columns across the width of the screen, enabling you to view more filenames.

To view a directory listing, one screen at a time:

❶ Type **DIR A: /P** and press **[Enter]**. DOS displays the first screen with part of the directory. See Figure 2-2. At the top of the screen, the DIR command displays the volume label. If you did not assign a volume label to the diskette when you format-ted it, the DIR command will tell you that the volume in the drive has no label. Next, you might see the diskette's serial number. On the third line, the DIR com-mand states that you are seeing a directory for a specific disk drive. At the bottom of this screen, DOS displays a prompt to press any key to continue.

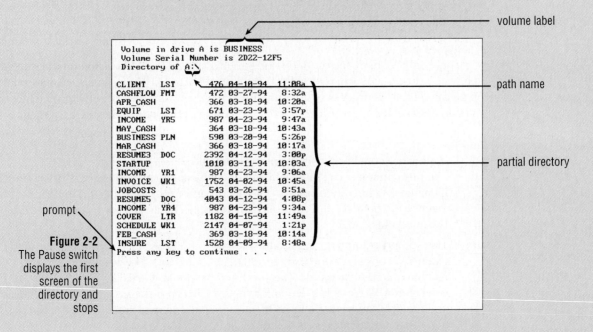

volume label

path name

partial directory

prompt

Figure 2-2
The Pause switch displays the first screen of the directory and stops

```
Volume in drive A is BUSINESS
Volume Serial Number is 2D22-12F5
Directory of A:\

CLIENT    LST      476 04-10-94   11:08a
CASHFLOW  FMT      472 03-27-94    8:32a
APR_CASH          366 03-18-94   10:20a
EQUIP     LST      671 03-23-94    3:57p
INCOME    YR5      987 04-23-94    9:47a
MAY_CASH          364 03-18-94   10:43a
BUSINESS  PLN      590 03-20-94    5:26p
MAR_CASH          366 03-18-94   10:17a
RESUME3   DOC     2392 04-12-94    3:00p
STARTUP          1010 03-11-94   10:03a
INCOME    YR1      987 04-23-94    9:06a
INVOICE   WK1     1752 04-02-94   10:45a
JOBCOSTS          543 03-26-94    8:51a
RESUME5   DOC     4043 04-12-94    4:08p
INCOME    YR4      987 04-23-94    9:34a
COVER     LTR     1182 04-15-94   11:49a
SCHEDULE  WK1     2147 04-07-94    1:21p
FEB_CASH          369 03-18-94   10:14a
INSURE    LST     1528 04-09-94    8:48a
Press any key to continue . . .
```

❷ Press **[Space]** or any other key to continue. DOS displays the second, and last, screen with the remainder of the directory. See Figure 2-3.

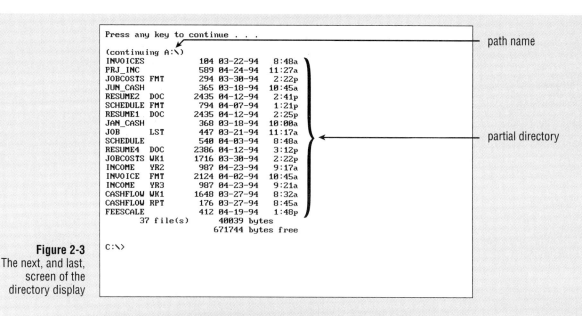

path name

partial directory

Figure 2-3
The next, and last, screen of the directory display

Next, you can view a wide directory listing.

③ Type **DIR A: /W** and press **[Enter]**. This directory listing shows all the files on your diskette on one screen. See Figure 2-4. You do not see the file size, date, and time, but the filenames are listed with a period between the main part of the filename and the file extension.

command

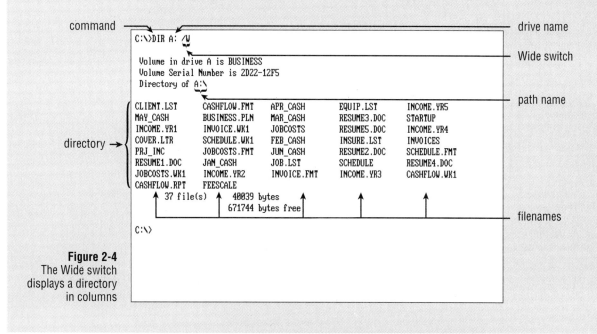

drive name

Wide switch

path name

directory

filenames

Figure 2-4
The Wide switch displays a directory in columns

The DIR command shows you a directory of the drive you specify. In the previous examples, you specified the name of the disk drive that contains your diskette. If you do not specify a drive name, DOS will look to the DOS prompt and display a directory of that drive. Many DOS commands operate in the same way.

To view a directory without specifying a drive:

① Type **A:**, or the drive name that contains your DOS Tutorials diskette, and press **[Enter]**. DOS updates the DOS prompt to show you the current drive.

② Type **DIR /P** and press **[Enter]**. Then press **[Space]** or any other key to view the next screen and to return to the DOS prompt. Again, you see a directory of your diskette one screen at a time, but you did not have to specify the drive. DOS uses the drive specified by the DOS prompt.

Next, you want to verify that your business partner included the file containing the business plan on the diskette. Because DOS does not display the directory in an order that makes it easy to find a file, you decide to use the **Order switch** (/O) which displays filenames in alphabetical order. You can also combine this switch with the Pause switch to view one screen at a time. Let's try it.

To display the directory in alphabetical order by filename, one screen at a time:

① Type **DIR /O /P** and press **[Enter]**. *Be sure you type the letter* "O" *and not a zero for the* Order switch. DOS displays the first screen of filenames in alphabetical order. See Figure 2-5. The second file, BUSINESS.PLN, is the one that you want to locate.

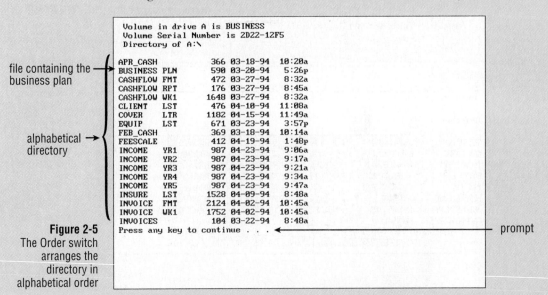

file containing the business plan →

alphabetical directory →

prompt

Figure 2-5
The Order switch arranges the directory in alphabetical order

```
Volume in drive A is BUSINESS
Volume Serial Number is 2D22-12F5
Directory of A:\

APR_CASH          366 03-18-94   10:20a
BUSINESS PLN      590 03-20-94    5:26p
CASHFLOW FMT      472 03-27-94    8:32a
CASHFLOW RPT      176 03-27-94    8:45a
CASHFLOW WK1     1648 03-27-94    8:32a
CLIENT   LST      476 04-10-94   11:08a
COVER    LTR     1182 04-15-94   11:49a
EQUIP    LST      671 03-23-94    3:57p
FEB_CASH          369 03-18-94   10:14a
FEESCALE          412 04-19-94    1:48p
INCOME   YR1      987 04-23-94    9:06a
INCOME   YR2      987 04-23-94    9:17a
INCOME   YR3      987 04-23-94    9:21a
INCOME   YR4      987 04-23-94    9:34a
INCOME   YR5      987 04-23-94    9:47a
INSURE   LST     1528 04-09-94    8:48a
INVOICE  FMT     2124 04-02-94   10:45a
INVOICE  WK1     1752 04-02-94   10:45a
INVOICES          104 03-22-94    8:48a
Press any key to continue . . .
```

② Press **[Space]** or any other key. DOS displays the filenames in the next, and last, screen in alphabetical order. Then DOS returns to the DOS prompt.

The DIR command is invaluable for identifying what files are stored on a diskette or for locating information on files. It is easy to forget which diskette contains a file that you need. This command is also useful when looking for a specific copy of a file; you can use the DIR command to check the dates and times of each version of a file to find the one you need.

Creating Files with the MS-DOS Editor

Your business partner has asked you to draft a short advertisement for your proposed business to include in the classified section of your local newspaper. You hope this ad will be the boost Professional Plus needs to attract potential clients. You decide to use a new feature in DOS 5.0 — the MS-DOS Editor. You can use this program to create documents composed of text. Not only can you enter text, but you can also **edit**, or modify, the text as you are working. For this reason, the feature is referred to as a **text editor**. Many software packages have text editors for creating small, simple documents. When you need to prepare more professional-looking, presentation-quality documents, you would use a word processing or desktop publishing program. The MS-DOS Editor will work well for the first draft of your business advertisement.

To start the MS-DOS Editor:

1. Be sure the current, or default, drive is the one with the DOS Tutorials diskette. The drive letter in the DOS prompt will show you the current drive. If necessary, type **A:** or **B:** to change to the drive with the DOS Tutorials diskette.

2. Type **EDIT** and press **[Enter]**. After the MS-DOS Editor is loaded into memory, you see its welcome screen. See Figure 2-6. You might notice that many of the elements in this screen are the same as in the Help screen you saw in Tutorial 1. If you experience difficulties starting or using the MS-DOS Editor, check with your instructor or a technical support person. DOS might be unable to locate the program and files it uses with the MS-DOS Editor.

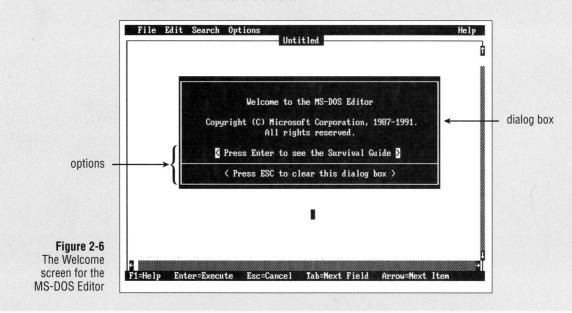

Figure 2-6
The Welcome screen for the MS-DOS Editor

The opening screen welcomes you to the MS-DOS Editor, displays copyright information, and gives you two options. One option tells you to press [Enter] to see the Survival Guide. The Survival Guide contains help information on the use of the MS-DOS Editor. The second option tells you to press [Esc] (Escape) to remove the dialog box from your screen.

The MS-DOS Editor uses **dialog boxes** to prompt for information, to list options, and to let you verify operations.

When you are using the MS-DOS Editor, or certain other programs included with DOS, you can use either the keyboard or the mouse to select program options. If you are using a mouse, read the next section. If you are not using a mouse, skip the next section.

Using the Mouse

A **mouse** is a hand-held device that moves a pointer around the screen in the direction that you move the mouse over a desk. The **mouse pointer** appears as a small rectangular box or as an arrow on the screen (see Figure 2-7). You use the mouse pointer to select an option displayed on the screen.

The following terms identify different types of operations you can perform with the mouse:

- When you **point** with the mouse, you move the mouse pointer so that it highlights a command, drive name, filename, **icon** (graphic image), or other object displayed on the screen or a specific area of the screen.

- When you **click** the left mouse button, you press then release it quickly. This feature permits you to select a command, drive name, filename, icon, or object on the screen or a specific area of the screen. Note that your mouse might include a right mouse button. When working in DOS, you use only the left mouse button.

- When you **double-click** the left mouse button, you quickly press it twice. If you want to select an option displayed on a screen that also contains text, you must double-click the option. Otherwise, if you click only once, you move the cursor.

- When you **shift-click**, you press and hold the Shift key and click the left mouse button. This feature allows you to select everything between the current cursor position and the location of the shift-click.

- When you **drag** the mouse, you hold down the left mouse button, move the mouse over an area, and then release the mouse button. You use this feature, for example, to select text or to select and move an object on the screen.

In some cases, you can perform operations more easily with the mouse than with the keyboard; in other instances, the keyboard is easier to use. You cannot use the mouse at the DOS prompt. This text gives you the instructions for using both the keyboard and the mouse to complete the steps.

Using the MS-DOS Editor's Survival Guide

You want to explore the Survival Guide so that you know how to find help information on the MS-DOS Editor. That way, if you have a problem while typing your advertisement, you'll know how to navigate around the MS-DOS Editor Help system to find the help you need.

To view the contents of the Survival Guide:

➊ With the cursor positioned on the first option, press **[Enter]**. If you are using the mouse, click the first option once with the left mouse button. The MS-DOS Editor displays a screen titled "HELP: Survival Guide." See Figure 2-7.

The Survival Guide provides a brief overview on using the MS-DOS Editor, and explains how to navigate around the MS-DOS Editor Help system. At the top of the screen is a *menu bar* with a list of menus. The *title bar* identifies the name of the current screen. The area below the title bar contains *help information*. The *status bar* at the bottom of the screen contains shortcut keys for performing specific operations.

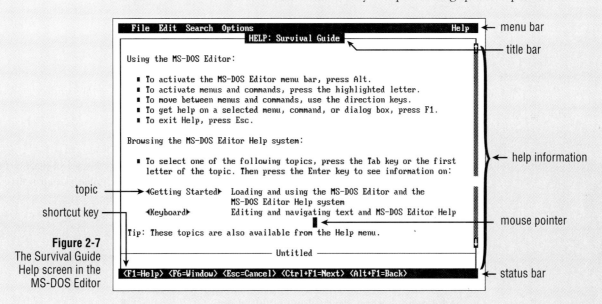

Figure 2-7
The Survival Guide
Help screen in the
MS-DOS Editor

➋ Be sure the cursor is on the option, or *topic*, entitled "Getting Started." If the cursor is on the topic "Keyboard," which explains how to use different types of keys, press [Tab] to return to the first topic. Then, press [Enter].

If you are using the mouse, double-click the option **Getting Started**. The MS-DOS Editor displays the Getting Started screen. See Figure 2-8 on the following page. There are three topics at the top of the screen and a set of more specific topics listed in the next area on the screen.

topics

specific topics

title bar

Figure 2-8
The Getting
Started Help
screen in the
MS-DOS Editor

③ Press **[Tab]** twice to move the cursor to the specific topic Using Help and press **[Enter]**. If you are using the mouse, double-click **Using Help**. The MS-DOS Editor displays the Using Help screen with general tips on how to use the Help feature in the MS-DOS Editor. See Figure 2-9.

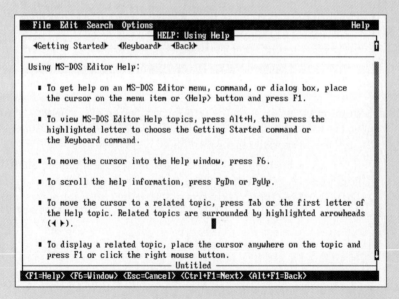

Figure 2-9
The Using Help
screen in the
MS-DOS Editor

④ Press **[Tab]** twice to move the cursor to Back and press **[Enter]**. If you are using the mouse, double-click **Back**. The MS-DOS Editor displays the previous screen. Press **[Tab]** to move the cursor to Back and press **[Enter]**, or double-click **Back** with the mouse. The MS-DOS Editor returns to the original screen.

⑤ Press **[Esc]**. If you are using the mouse, click **Esc=Cancel** in the status bar. The Help screen disappears and you see the main editing screen where you enter and edit text. See Figure 2-10. *You can exit the Help system from any screen by pressing [Esc].*

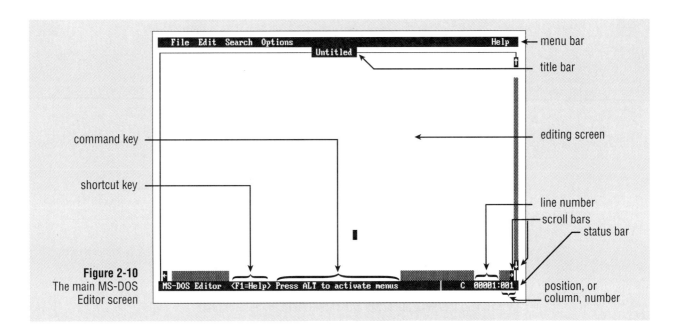

Figure 2-10
The main MS-DOS
Editor screen

The editing screen contains a menu bar listing the menus you can use as you create a document. The title bar is currently labeled "Untitled." After you name a file, you will see the filename displayed in the title bar. The editing screen is empty. The information on the status bar has changed. The shortcut key tells you that if you want to access Help at any point, you press [F1] (Help). If you want to access the menu bar, the command key tells you to press [Alt] (Menu). The current coordinates of the cursor are shown at the right end of the status bar. The first five digits tell you the line number where the cursor is positioned. The three digits after the colon tell you what the position of the cursor is on a line. Right now, the cursor is at the first position (or first column) on the first line. If you are using a mouse, you can adjust the screen view with the **scroll bars**. The scroll bars include the vertical bar on the right side of the screen and the horizontal bar at the bottom of the screen.

Creating a File with the MS-DOS Editor

You are now ready to enter the draft of your business advertisement. To enter text, you just start typing.

To enter the draft of your business advertisement:

❶ Press **[Tab]**. The cursor moves to the right eight positions. When you print this file, the text will print approximately one inch from the left edge of the paper.

❷ Press **[Caps Lock]** once so that you can enter the title of the advertisement in upper-case. The Caps Lock indicator light on the keyboard should now be on. If this light is off, press [Caps Lock] again. [Caps Lock] is a toggle key. A *toggle key* switches, or alternates, between two related uses each time you press the key.

③   Type **BUSINESS AD** and press **[Caps Lock]** to return to lowercase. Then, press **[Enter]** three times to end the first line and leave two blank lines after the title. The MS-DOS Editor automatically indents the cursor so that it lines up with the "B" in "BUSINESS." This feature is called *auto-indent*. It saves you time and effort, and is very useful when you need to indent a document consistently or prepare an outline.

④   Type the following line of text:

Professionally prepared documents for business, finac

You realize that you have made a typing error.

⑤   Press **[Backspace]** once to delete the "c." Then, type **ncial, job** and press **[Enter]** twice. You want a double-spaced draft so that you and your business partner can edit it easily.

⑥   As you type the remaining text, press **[Enter]** twice to insert a blank line between each line:

search, and personal use. Laser printing; fax service; copy

service. Reasonable costs and turnaround times. Contact

Professional Plus at 777-7777 for an estimate.

⑦   Press **[Enter]** after you type the last line.

After entering this text, you decide to make two small changes. You want to change the word "costs" to "fees" so that the ad sounds more professional. Also, you want to insert the word "quick" before the word "turnaround" to emphasize your business response time.

To edit the business ad:

①   Press **[↑]** until the cursor is positioned on the line that starts with the word "service." Then, press **[→]** until the cursor is positioned on the "c" in the word "costs." If you are using the mouse, click the **c** in "costs." When you move the mouse pointer and then click, the cursor moves to that position in the document.

②   Press **[Del]** four times. If you are using the mouse, click the **c** and hold the left mouse button. Then, drag the mouse to the right to select the characters **cost**. As you select these characters, they will appear highlighted. Then, release the left mouse button and press **[Del]**. The MS-DOS Editor deletes the characters "cost" and closes up the text.

③   Type **fee** and note that the MS-DOS Editor automatically inserts these characters at the position of the cursor.

④   Press **[→]** until the cursor is positioned on the "t" in "turnaround." If you are using the mouse, click the **t** in "turnaround."

⑤   Type **quick** and press **[Space]**. The MS-DOS Editor inserts this word. Figure 2-11 shows the revised and completed business advertisement.

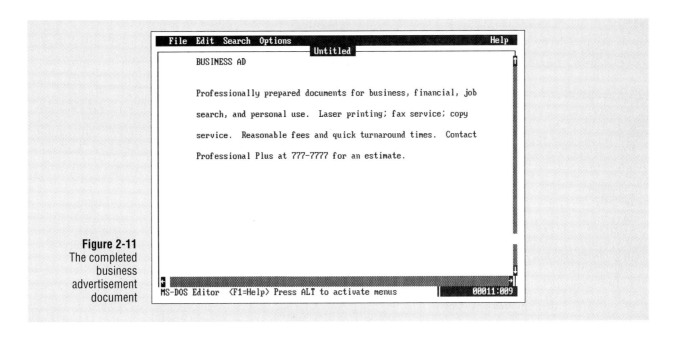

Figure 2-11
The completed
business
advertisement
document

Saving a File Created with the MS-DOS Editor

Now that you have created the first draft of your business ad, you should save your work. It is a good idea to save your work frequently as you use a computer. Your document is currently stored in RAM, which is volatile. If the power fails, or if you experience some other problem that requires you to perform a cold boot or a warm boot, you will lose your work. However, if you save your work and then a problem occurs, you can retrieve a copy of the document and continue working.

When you issue a command to a program to save the document that you are working on, the program, in conjunction with DOS, stores a copy of this document in a file on a diskette or hard disk (Figure 2-12). That copy on disk is a "snapshot" of the current document you are using.

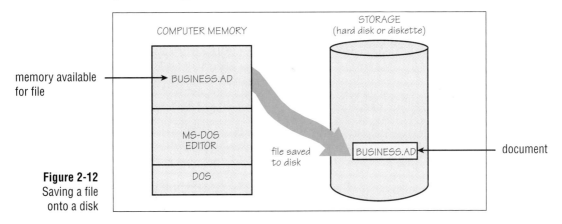

memory available
for file

document

Figure 2-12
Saving a file
onto a disk

To record a copy of your document from RAM onto your DOS Tutorials diskette:

① Press **[Alt]** to access the menu bar. The first menu, File, is highlighted. One letter in each menu is highlighted. To select a menu, you can type that letter, or you can press [Enter] to select the highlighted menu.

② Type **F** (or press [Enter]) to select the File menu. If you are using the mouse, click the **File** menu. The MS-DOS Editor displays a drop-down menu with a list of commands. See Figure 2-13. You see two commands for saving a file, but you are not sure which one you should use.

currently selected menu

Save and Save As commands

drop-down menu listing commands

highlighted command

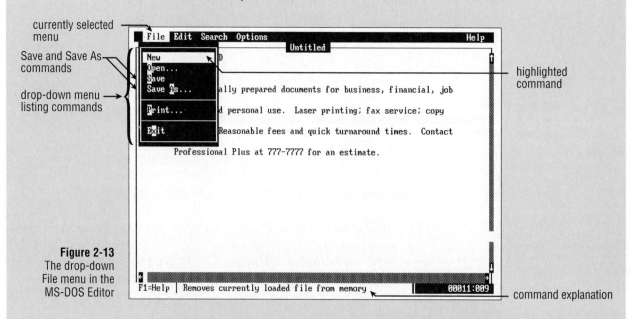

Figure 2-13
The drop-down File menu in the MS-DOS Editor

command explanation

③ Press **[↓]** twice to highlight Save. On the status bar, the MS-DOS Editor tells you that this command "Saves current file." Because you have not yet named the file, you decide to check the next command.

④ Press **[↓]** to highlight Save As. The MS-DOS Editor informs you that this command "Saves current file with specified name." This is the command you need.

⑤ Press **[Enter]** to select the highlighted Save As command. If you are using the mouse, click the **Save As** command. The Save As dialog box appears. See Figure 2-14.

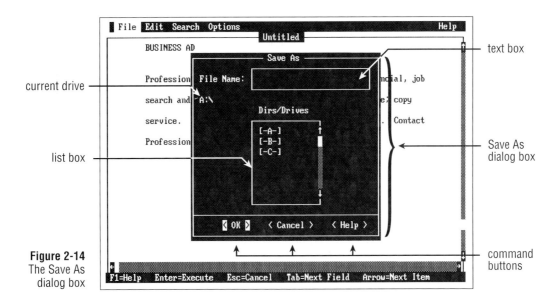

Figure 2-14
The Save As
dialog box

The cursor is positioned in the first box, next to the File Name prompt. This box is called a **text box**. Below this box the MS-DOS Editor displays the current drive. In the box labeled Dirs/Drives, the MS-DOS Editor displays the disk drives available on your computer system. The names of directories on your hard drive might also be listed in this text box. This second type of box is called a **list box** because it contains a list of items from which you can choose. At the bottom of this dialog box are the OK, Cancel, and Help command buttons. Selecting OK tells DOS to execute the command, or save the file with the selected name. You select Cancel if you've made a mistake and don't want to save the file. If you select the Help button, the MS-DOS Editor will provide help information on the Save As command. You decide to name this file BUSINESS AD.

To assign a filename to the document and save it to disk:

1. Press **[Tab]** to move the cursor to the Dirs/Drive list box. Use the **[↓]** to highlight the drive that contains your DOS Tutorials diskette. Drive names appear in brackets. If you are using the mouse, click the drive name. The MS-DOS Editor highlights the drive name you selected. Be sure to select the correct drive for saving the file to your DOS Tutorials diskette. If not, you might accidentally save the file to the hard drive or another disk drive.

2. Press **[Enter]** to select the drive name and return to the File Name text box. A highlighted asterisk (*) appears indicating that you can use any filename. If you are using the mouse the drive name will appear in the File Name text box. Click in the File Name text box to select this box. You can now enter the filename. As you type it in, it replaces the contents of the box.

3. Type **BUSINESS AD** and press **[Enter]**. The MS-DOS Editor displays the Bad file name dialog box. See Figure 2-15 on the following page. DOS will not accept this filename because it contains 11 characters and a space. Filenames cannot be longer than eight characters and cannot contain any spaces. You could use the filename "BUSINESS.AD."

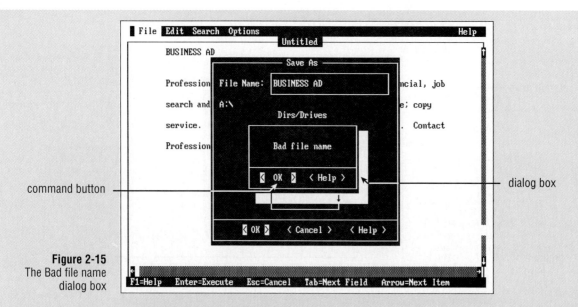

command button ──

── dialog box

Figure 2-15
The Bad file name
dialog box

④ Press **[Enter]** to select OK. If you are using the mouse, click **OK**. The cursor returns to the File Name text box.

⑤ Press **[←]** three times to position the cursor on the blank space, press **[Ins]** (Insert), type **[.]** (period), and press **[Enter]**. [Ins] is a toggle key that switches between insert mode and replace (or typeover) mode. If you are using the mouse, click the blank space between BUSINESS and AD, press **[Ins]**, type **[.]** (period), and click **OK**. The MS-DOS Editor saves the document with the filename BUSINESS.AD on your DOS Tutorials diskette. The dialog box disappears and you return to the editing window. The filename is now shown in the title bar. See Figure 2-16 .

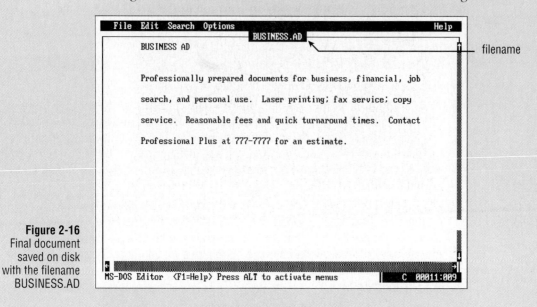

── filename

Figure 2-16
Final document
saved on disk
with the filename
BUSINESS.AD

Opening an Existing File

You want to examine the contents of the file that contains the business plan. You and your partner had discussed the importance of including sections that summarize your financial goals and marketing strategy before applying for a business loan at your local bank. You want to be sure that your partner included this information in the revised outline for the business plan.

To open the file containing the business plan:

1. Press **[Alt]** and then press **[Enter]** to select the File menu. If you are using the mouse, click **File**.

2. Press **[↓]** to point to Open. On the status bar, the MS-DOS Editor informs you that this command "Loads new file into memory." This is the command you need.

3. Press **[Enter]**, or click **Open** with the mouse. The MS-DOS Editor displays the Open dialog box. See Figure 2-17. In the File Name text box, the MS-DOS Editor displays *.TXT — a notation indicating that DOS will automatically display a list of all files with the extension TXT (an abbreviation for text) in the Files box when you select OK. The MS-DOS Editor assumes that any file you create will have this descriptive extension. Because no files on your DOS Tutorials diskette have this extension, the Files box is empty.

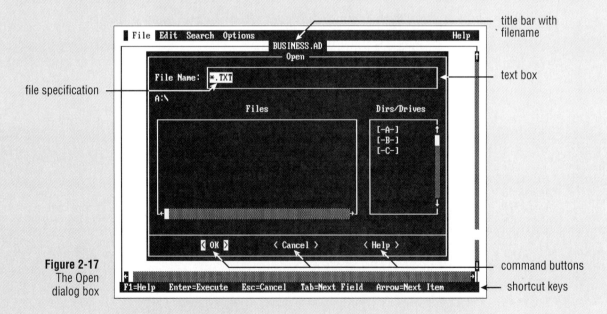

Figure 2-17
The Open
dialog box

4. Press **[Tab]** to move the cursor to the Dirs/Drive list box, or click in the **Dirs/Drive** box with the mouse. There might be more drives listed on your computer system than in Figure 2-17.

5. Use the **[↓]** to highlight the drive that contains your DOS Tutorials diskette. To select a drive with the mouse, click the drive name.

⑥   Press **[Enter]** to select the drive with your DOS Tutorials diskette. If you are using the mouse, click anywhere in the File Name text box. The cursor returns to this box.

⑦   Type **BUSINESS.PLN** and press **[Enter]**. The MS-DOS Editor retrieves a copy of this file from your diskette. The screen view shows part of the outline for the business plan.

⑧   Press **[PgDn]** to view the next screen. The MS-DOS Editor adjusts the screen view so that you can see the next part of the file. Depending on your hardware, you might see different lines. If you are using the mouse, you can drag the scroll box down the scroll bar to adjust the screen view. The scroll bars include the vertical bar on the right side of the screen and the horizontal bar at the bottom of the screen. The *scroll box* is the small box on a scroll bar that indicates your relative position within the document. If you drag the scroll box to a new position on the scroll bar, the screen view changes to show another section of the document. Each scroll bar also contains *scroll arrows* that indicate the directions in which you can adjust the screen view onto the document. You can click one of the arrows on the vertical scroll bar to view the previous line or the next line.

⑨   Press **[↑]** five times to view the previous five lines. See Figure 2-18. If you are using the mouse, you can drag the scroll box a short distance. Again, the screen scrolls so that you can see another view of the document.

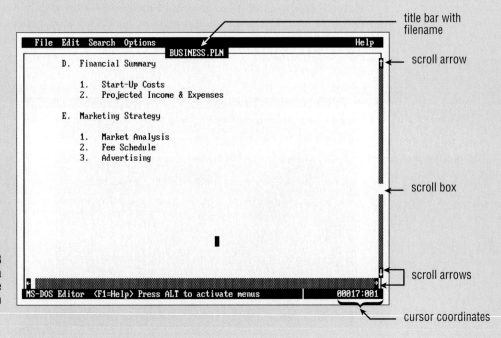

Figure 2-18
A view of a
portion of the
business plan

The outline for the business plan includes sections for your financial goals and market analysis. Now that you have found the information you wanted to verify, you are ready to exit the MS-DOS Editor.

To exit the MS-DOS Editor:

① Press **[Alt]** and then press **[Enter]** to select the File menu. If you are using the mouse, click **File**.

② Press **[↓]** five times to select the Exit command. Then, press **[Enter].** If you are using the mouse, click **Exit**. You exit the MS-DOS Editor and return to the DOS prompt. If a dialog box appears asking if you want to save your changes, the MS-DOS Editor assumes that you made some change to the document, or simply pressed a key. For example, you might have pressed [Space]. If this occurs, press [Tab] to select No and press [Enter]. If you are using the mouse, click No.

If you want to take a break, make sure you remove all diskettes from the computer before leaving. If you are working in a lab, ask your instructor or technical support person whether it is necessary to turn off the computer. If so, locate the power switch and turn it to the "OFF" position. Then, locate the power switch to the monitor and turn off the power. If you want to continue, go on to the next section.

Viewing the Contents of a Text File

You want to view the contents of the file that contains the fee scale developed by your business partner. This file, and many of the other files on your diskette, are ASCII files. An **ASCII file** is a simple file format in which information is stored as text. The name ASCII stands for **A**merican **S**tandard **C**ode for **I**nformation **I**nterchange. Different companies in the computer industry recognize this standard coding format for storing information in a file. The terms **DOS files**, **DOS text files**, or **text files** are also used to refer to ASCII files. You can use the TYPE command to display the contents of a text file on the screen. You do not need to start a program and then retrieve a file to view its contents.

You cannot use the TYPE command to view the contents of a program file or a file produced by an application like Lotus 1-2-3. If you do, DOS attempts to interpret the file's contents and displays unintelligible symbols on the screen.

To view the contents of the text file containing fee information:

① Type **TYPE A:FEESCALE** and press **[Enter]**. DOS displays the contents of the text file on the screen. See Figure 2-19 on the following page. The fee scale reflects the current rates for work in your business region.

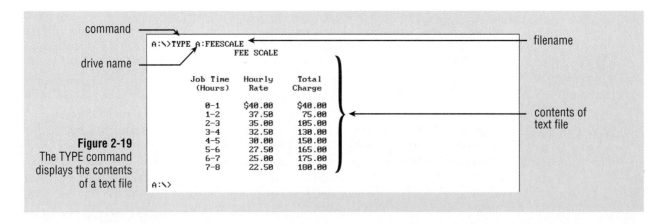

Figure 2-19
The TYPE command displays the contents of a text file

Now that you are familiar with entering commands at the DOS prompt, you are ready to learn a more visual approach for interacting with DOS. Your business partner tells you about the DOS Shell and explains that it is easy to work with and can save you time.

Using the DOS Shell

The DOS Shell allows you to work with DOS in a more visual way than is possible when working at the DOS prompt. The DOS Shell displays information on disk drives, directories, files, and programs. It also contains its own menu system so that you can select DOS commands from a menu, rather than type them at the DOS prompt. In this way, it is similar to the MS-DOS Editor. Like a desktop, the DOS Shell contains all the tools you need to work with DOS and your computer system.

You decide to compare the use of the DOS Shell with the use of commands at the DOS prompt so that you and your business partner can choose the most effective and efficient way to work on your computer systems to complete business contracts.

To access the DOS Shell:

❶ Be sure the current drive contains the DOS Tutorials diskette. If necessary, change drives.

❷ Type **DOSSHELL** (as one word with no spaces) and press **[Enter]**. After DOS loads the DOS Shell program into the computer's memory, you will see the DOS Shell. See Figure 2-20. Because there are different ways to customize the screen view of the DOS Shell, your view might be different from the one in the figure. If you are unable to access the DOS Shell, or if your screen looks different from the screen in Figure 2-20, check with your instructor or technical support person.

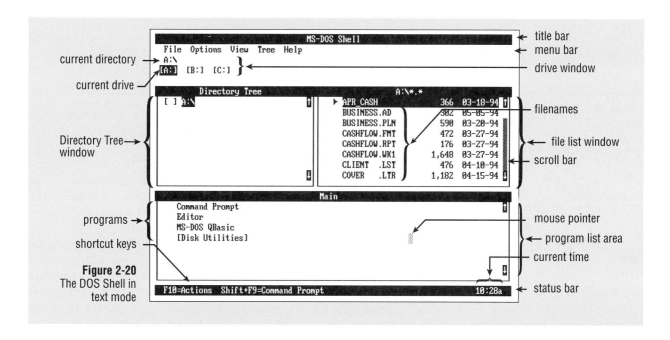

Figure 2-20
The DOS Shell in
text mode

The view of the DOS Shell shown in Figure 2-20 is referred to as **text mode**. In text mode, DOS uses standard keyboard characters and symbols to represent diskettes, files, and programs. When you install DOS, the DOS Shell is automatically installed in text mode. You can also customize the DOS Shell so that it is displayed in **graphics mode**. See Figure 2-21. In graphics mode, DOS Shell uses **icons** — graphical images or pictures — to represent diskettes, files, and programs.

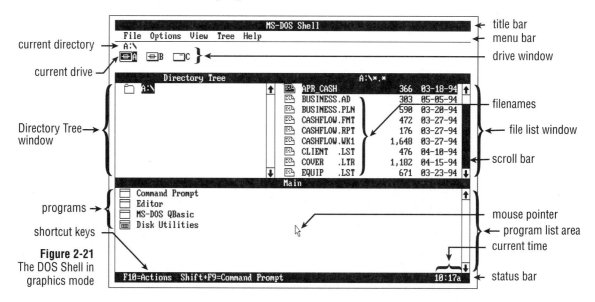

Figure 2-21
The DOS Shell in
graphics mode

The DOS Shell screen is divided into different areas, or **windows**. These can also be customized. If your screen looks different from Figure 2-20 or 2-21, see you instructor or technical support person for help returning it to the **default setting**, or the setting automatically installed with DOS. At the top of the screen is the title bar with the title **MS-DOS Shell**.

The menu bar on the next line contains the following menus: File, Options, View, Tree, and Help. It looks similar to the menu bar in the MS-DOS Editor.

The **drive window**, located immediately below the menu bar, shows the current directory and the drives available on your computer system. If your computer system contains a hard drive and two diskette drives, the DOS Shell will list drives A, B, and C. If you are using a network, the DOS Shell will also list network drives, such as drive F, G, or H. The DOS Shell highlights the current drive. One of the advantages of using the DOS Shell is that you know what drives are included on your computer system.

The DOS Shell uses the Directory Tree window to represent the organization of files on a diskette or hard disk. On your diskette, all the files are stored in the root directory of the diskette. The **root directory** is the first and most important directory on a diskette. The FORMAT command creates the root directory of a diskette. The **file list window** shows the files on your diskette. The filenames are automatically listed in alphabetical order.

The window at the bottom of the screen, with the title **Main**, is called the **program list area**. This window displays the list of programs that you can access from the DOS Shell. The Command Prompt program allows you to temporarily exit to the DOS prompt. The Editor program allows you to use the MS-DOS Editor from the DOS Shell. The MS-DOS QBasic program allows you to use the Quick BASIC programming language included with DOS. The Disk Utilities program provides a group of utility commands, such as the one for formatting diskettes, that you can execute from the DOS Shell. You can add software applications such as WordPerfect 5.1 or Lotus 1-2-3 to this list so that you can use them directly from the DOS Shell. This feature allows you to organize and access all the programs you commonly use on your computer system.

Below the Main window is the status bar. The status bar displays the shortcut keys for [F10] (Actions) and [Shift][F9] (Command Prompt) as well as the current time.

As you work in a window, your reference point is a **selection cursor** that highlights a drive, directory name, filename, or program name. When you first start the DOS Shell, this selection cursor identifies the current drive. The selection cursor is a special type of cursor used in the DOS Shell.

When you meet with your business partner, you want to decide on insurance coverage and finalize the business advertisement. You want to view the contents of these two files before the meeting.

To view the contents of the two files:

1. Press **[Tab]** twice to move the selection cursor to the file list window. If you are using the mouse, click in the file list window.

2. Type **I** to quickly move the selection cursor to the first file that starts with the letter "I." Then, press **[↓]** five times and highlight the file named INSURE.LST. If you are using the mouse, click the **[↓]** on the vertical scroll bar to the right of the filenames until you see the filename INSURE.LST. Click the filename **INSURE.LST**.

3. Press **[F10]** to access the menu bar. Press **[Enter]** to select the File menu. If you are using the mouse, click the **File** menu. The DOS Shell displays the drop-down File menu. See Figure 2-22.

currently → selected menu

drop-down → menu

Figure 2-22
The drop-down
File menu in the
DOS Shell

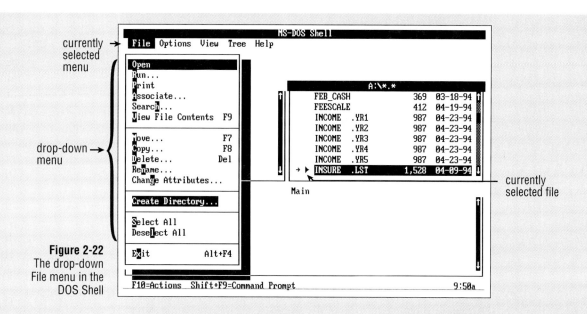

currently selected file

Press [↓] five times to highlight the View File Contents command. Then, press **[Enter]**. If you are using the mouse, click the **View File Contents** command. Note that you can also press [F9] (View) to issue the command. The DOS Shell displays part of the file. See Figure 2-23. The number of lines that you see on your screen might be different. Note that this screen has its own title bar, menu bar, and status bar. It also provides information on how to use scrolling keys to view the rest of the file.

partial contents
of text file →

Figure 2-23
The View File
Contents command
displays the contents
of the text file

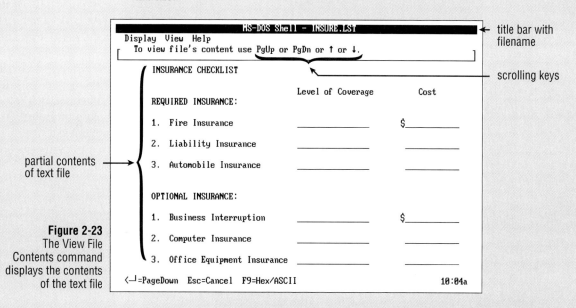

title bar with filename

scrolling keys

Press **[Esc]**. If you are using the mouse, click the **View** menu and then click the **Restore View** command. You return to the main DOS Shell screen.

Type **B** to move the selection cursor to the first filename that starts with the letter B — BUSINESS.AD. Then press **[F9]** to view the contents of the business ad you prepared with the MS-DOS Editor. Then press **[Esc]** to exit.

⑦ Press **[F10]** and press **[Enter]** to select the File menu. Then, type **X** to select the Exit command. If you are using the mouse, click the **File** menu and then click the **Exit** command. The fastest way to exit the DOS Shell is to press [F3].

The DOS Shell provides you with easy access to different types of information stored on your computer — an important factor in the daily operation and success of your business. Furthermore, it provides a logical, friendly, and professional approach to the use of computers.

Printing a Text File

You're ready to submit an application for a business loan to your local bank. You need to include a printed copy of the outline of your business plan as a cover sheet to the application.

You can use the PRINT command to print a copy of a text file. When you use this command, DOS prompts you for the name of your printer port. A **port** is a connection between your computer system and another hardware component, such as a printer. Just as DOS assigns names to each of the disk drives, it also assigns names to each of the ports on your computer system. Because it is possible to connect more than one printer to a computer system, DOS assigns the name PRN (an abbreviation for printer) to the first printer port on your computer system. The other port names are LPT1 (an abbreviation for line printer 1), LPT2, LPT3, COM1 (an abbreviation for communications port 1), COM2, COM3, and COM4. In most cases, you can specify PRN or LPT1 as the printer port and DOS will know which port to use.

To print a copy of the business plan:
① Be sure the printer is on. If the printer is off, turn on the ON/OFF switch.
② Be sure the printer has paper and that the paper is properly aligned.
③ Be sure the printer is *on-line*, or capable of receiving output from the computer. Most printers have an On Line button. If the light next to the On Line button is on, the printer is ready to receive information from the computer. If the light next to the On Line button is off, the printer is *off-line*, or unable to receive information from the computer. If the printer is off-line, press the On Line button once. It functions like a toggle key.
④ At the DOS prompt, type **PRINT A:BUSINESS.PLN** and press **[Enter]**. DOS prompts you for the name of the list device. A *list device* is a printer port.
⑤ Press **[Enter]** to accept the default list device, PRN. DOS loads the PRINT program into memory and informs you that the file is currently being printed. If the printer does not print the file, or if DOS displays an error message, check with your instructor or technical support person. You might need to specify the name of another printer port or check the status of the printer.
⑥ Remove your printed copy of the business plan from the printer.

Next, you want to use the DOS Shell to print a copy of the business advertisement. Before you can print from the DOS Shell you must issue the PRINT command at the DOS prompt.

This is the only DOS command that requires this extra step. Because you have already performed this step, the PRINT program is still stored in RAM and you can use it in the DOS Shell.

To print the file with the business advertisement from the DOS Shell:

❶ Type **DOSSHELL** and press **[Enter]**.

❷ Press **[Tab]** twice to move the selection cursor to the file list window. If you are using the mouse, click in the file list window.

❸ Press **[↓]** to highlight the file named BUSINESS.AD. If you are using the mouse, click the filename **BUSINESS.AD**.

❹ Press **[F10]**, and then press **[Enter]** to select the File menu. Press **[↓]** twice to highlight the Print command, and press **[Enter]**. If you are using the mouse, click the **File** menu, then click the **Print** command. The DOS Shell relays a request to the PRINT program to print a copy of the selected file.

❺ Remove your printed copy of the business advertisement from the printer.

❻ Press **[F3]** to exit the DOS Shell.

Using Wildcards with the DIR Command

The diskette provided by your business partner now contains 38 files. You expect the number to increase as your business gets underway. When you need to use a group of files, you want to be able to select them without having to view the names of all the other files on the diskette. To simplify the process of selecting files with similar filenames, you can use **wildcards** to substitute for part or all of a filename. There are two wildcard characters — the question mark and the asterisk. The **question mark** (?) substitutes for one character in a filename and the **asterisk** (*) substitutes for one or more characters.

You will use the wildcards to select the files containing the **templates**, or document formats, for preparing resumes and for monitoring cash flow. These files are going to be used and updated constantly in your business. You can also combine wildcards with switches to improve the results of your selections.

To select the template files using wildcards and switches:

❶ Type **DIR A:RESUME? /O** and press **[Enter]**. If your diskette is in drive B, substitute that drive name for drive A in the command. DOS displays an alphabetical directory with five files — RESUME1.DOC, RESUME2.DOC, RESUME3.DOC, RESUME4.DOC, and RESUME5.DOC. See Figure 2-24 on the following page. DOS substituted the question mark with any character in the seventh position of the file-name. Note that if the current drive is the one with your DOS Tutorials diskette, you do not need to specify the drive name. In other words, you can type DIR RESUME? /O and get the same result.

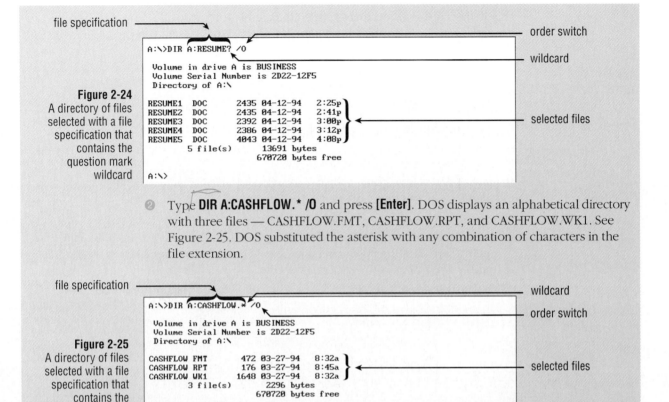

file specification
order switch
wildcard

Figure 2-24
A directory of files
selected with a file
specification that
contains the
question mark
wildcard

selected files

file specification
wildcard
order switch

Figure 2-25
A directory of files
selected with a file
specification that
contains the
asterisk wildcard

selected files

② Type **DIR A:CASHFLOW.* /O** and press **[Enter]**. DOS displays an alphabetical directory
with three files — CASHFLOW.FMT, CASHFLOW.RPT, and CASHFLOW.WK1. See
Figure 2-25. DOS substituted the asterisk with any combination of characters in the
file extension.

③ Type **DIR A:*.* /O /P** and press **[Enter]**. DOS displays an alphabetical directory of all
the files on the diskette, one screen at a time. DOS substituted the asterisks in the
selection (pronounced "star-dot-star") with any combination of characters in the
main part of the filename and in the file extension.

Wildcards and switches can be combined in different ways, depending on the type of
filenames that you want to select and how you want to display them on the screen. Next,
you decide to use the DOS Shell to check for the files that contain important checklists for
starting your business and the files for preparing invoices.

To view a directory of selected files using the DOS Shell:

① Be sure the current drive is the one with your DOS Tutorials diskette.

② If DOSKEY is installed, press **[↑]** to search through the DOS commands until you find
DOSSHELL. If you can't find it, type **DOSSHELL** and press **[Enter]**. DOSKEY saves
you from retyping the same commands.

③ Press **[F10]** to access the menu bar, press **[→]** to highlight Options, and press **[Enter]**.
If you are using the mouse, click **Options**.

④ Press **[↓]** to highlight File Display Options and press **[Enter]**. If you are using the
mouse, click **File Display Options**. The DOS Shell displays the File Display Options

dialog box. See Figure 2-26. The Name field shows the current type of file selection — *.* (star-dot-star) for all files. The dialog box provides options for displaying hidden files and system files. *Hidden files* are files that are not displayed in a directory. *System files* are the DOS program files. System files are also hidden to protect them.

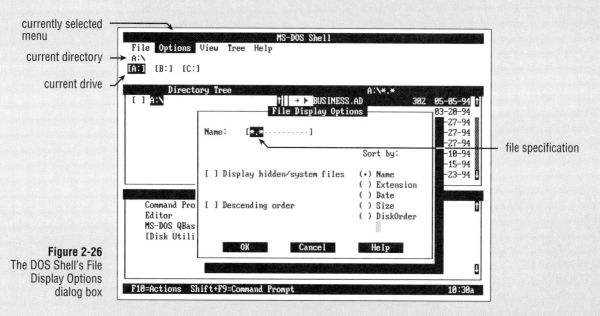

currently selected menu

current directory

current drive

file specification

Figure 2-26
The DOS Shell's File Display Options dialog box

⑤ Type ***.LST** and press **[Enter]** to replace *.*. DOS updates the file list window to show an alphabetical directory of four files — CLIENT.LST, EQUIP.LST, INSURE.LST, and JOB.LST. See Figure 2-27. DOS substituted the asterisk with any combination of characters in the main part of the filename.

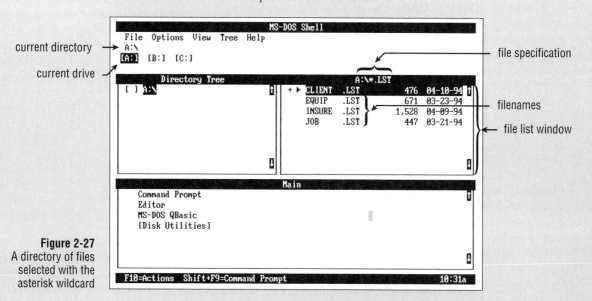

current directory

current drive

file specification

filenames

file list window

Figure 2-27
A directory of files selected with the asterisk wildcard

⑥ Press **[F10]** to access the menu bar, press **[→]** to highlight Options, and press **[Enter]**. If you are using the mouse, click **Options**.

⑦ Press **[↓]** to highlight File Display Options and press **[Enter]**. If you are using the mouse, click **File Display Options**.

⑧ Type **INV*** and press **[Enter]**. DOS updates the file list window to show an alphabetical directory with three files — INVOICE.FMT, INVOICE.WK1, and INVOICES. See Figure 2-28. DOS substituted the asterisk with any combination of characters in the main part of the filename after the letters INV. DOS includes files with and without a file extension.

current directory

current drive

file specification

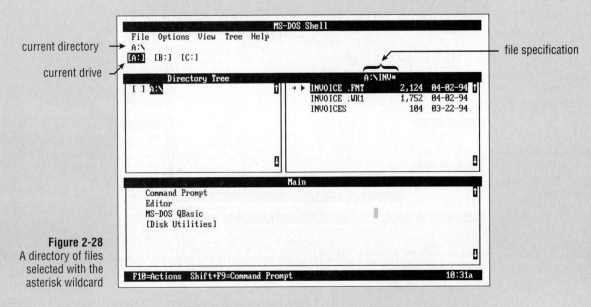

Figure 2-28
A directory of files selected with the asterisk wildcard

⑨ Press **[F3]** to exit the DOS Shell.

Wildcards are useful for producing directories of selected files either from the DOS prompt or from the DOS Shell. You can also use wildcards with other DOS commands so that you can perform operations on groups of files.

Before you begin the next section, you might want to take a break. Make sure you remove all diskettes from the computer before leaving. If you're working in a lab, ask your instructor or technical support person whether it is necessary to turn off the computer. If so, locate the power switch and turn it to the "OFF" position. Then, locate the power switch to the monitor and turn off the power.

Copying Files

Next, you want to make a copy of the file that contains a resume so that you can produce a new version of that resume format. With these templates, you and your business partner will be able to quickly prepare final copies of resumes while a client supplies you with the necessary information. The fast turnaround times will give your new business an edge in the marketplace.

You can use the COPY command to copy the contents of an existing file into a new file on the same diskette (Figure 2-29). The general syntax for the COPY command is as follows:

COPY *source target*

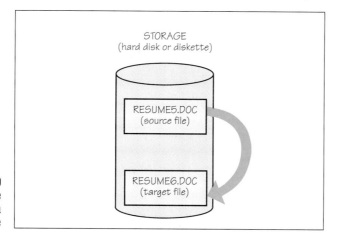

Figure 2-29
Copying a file to the same diskette with a new filename

The file that you copy is the **source file** — in this case, RESUME5.DOC. The new file that you produce from the copy operation is the **target file**, or destination file — in this case, RESUME6.DOC. Depending on where you copy the file from and to, you might need to specify all or part of the path name for each file. The full path name includes the disk drive name, the directory name, and the filename.

Before you make a copy of a file, you should use the DIR command to verify that you do not have a file with the same name as the one that you intend to use for the new file. You know that you have several resume files and that you have named them in consecutive order — RESUME1.DOC, RESUME2.DOC, etc. You want to name this file RESUME6.DOC, but you need to make sure that this file doesn't already exist. Your partner might have added an extra resume file to this diskette. If you use an existing filename, DOS will copy over that file without warning you, and you will lose that file's contents. After you make a copy of a file, you should verify that the copy operation worked.

To copy the file containing the format for preparing a resume:

① Be sure the current drive is the one with your DOS Tutorials diskette. If this is not the case, you *must* specify the drive name for the source and target files.

② Type **DIR RESUME? /O** and press **[Enter]** to check that you do not have a file named RESUME6.DOC. DOS assumes you want to use the current drive and that you want to include any file extension.

③ Type **COPY A:RESUME5.DOC A:RESUME6.DOC** and press **[Enter]**. If you are using drive B, substitute that drive name for drive A in the command. DOS displays the message "1 file(s) copied" and then displays the DOS prompt again. If you do not specify a drive, DOS uses the current drive. To save keystroking, you can omit the drive names if the files are on the diskette in the current drive.

Now you should check that the new file exists.

④ Type **DIR RESUME? /O** and press **[Enter]**. The file RESUME6.DOC is shown in the directory. See Figure 2-30 on the following page.

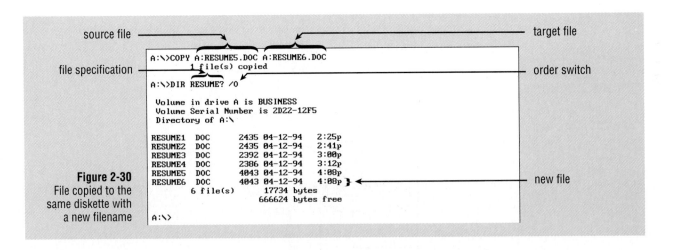

Figure 2-30
File copied to the
same diskette with
a new filename

During the first years of your business, you and your business partner expect to work
on the computer systems in your office as well as those in your homes. You plan to have
two computers in your office: one with a 3½-inch high-density drive, and one with a 5¼-inch
high-density drive. Your computer at home has a 3½-inch high-density drive, whereas your
business partner has a computer with a 5¼-inch high-density drive. You will need to know
how to copy from one disk drive to another as well as to, and from, a hard disk drive.

The next three sections describe how to copy files from one drive to another from the
DOS prompt. Complete the section that applies to the type of computer you are using.

Copying a File Using One Disk Drive

If you have a single disk drive, you can copy from one diskette to another diskette using the
same drive. DOS treats this disk drive as drive A *and* drive B. If your computer has two disk
drives, skip to the next section.

You want to copy the file RESUME6.DOC from your DOS Tutorials diskette to your DOS
Exercises diskette.

To copy a file to another diskette on a computer system with only one disk drive:

❶ Remove your DOS Tutorials diskette, and insert your DOS Exercises diskette into the
disk drive. Make sure drive A is the current drive.

❷ Type **DIR RESUME? /O** and press **[Enter]** to verify that you do not have a file named
RESUME6.DOC on your DOS Exercises diskette.

❸ Remove your DOS Exercises diskette and insert your DOS Tutorials diskette into the
disk drive.

❹ Type **COPY RESUME6.DOC B:** and press **[Enter]**. After DOS copies the file, it prompts
you to insert the diskette for drive B, the target diskette, and to press any key when
ready.

❺ Insert your DOS Exercises diskette and press **[Space]** or any other key. You should
see the message "1 file(s) copied." See Figure 2-31. DOS copies the file to this diskette and prompts you to insert the diskette for drive A, the source diskette, and
press any key when ready.

```
A:\>COPY RESUME6.DOC B:

Insert diskette for drive B: and press any key when ready

        1 file(s) copied


Insert diskette for drive A: and press any key when ready
```

Figure 2-31
Copying a file to
another diskettte
using one drive

⑥ Insert your DOS Tutorials diskette and press **[Space]** or any other key. DOS displays the DOS prompt.

⑦ Remove your DOS Tutorials diskette, and insert your DOS Exercises diskette.

Now you need to verify that the copy operation worked.

⑧ Type **DIR RESUME? /O** and press **[Enter]**. You should see RESUME6.DOC in the directory listing.

Copying a File Using Two Disk Drives

You want to copy the file with the business advertisement from your DOS Tutorials diskette to a blank, formatted diskette to send to the newspaper. If you have two disk drives, you can copy a file from one diskette to another, even if the diskettes are different sizes and have different storage capacities (Figure 2-32). To complete this section, you need a blank, formatted diskette that matches the size of one of the disk drives on your computer. *See page DOS 20 for instructions on how to format a diskette.*

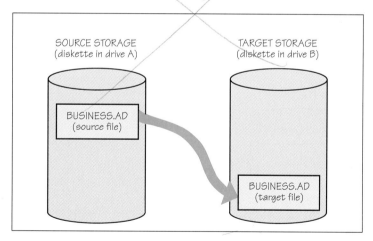

Figure 2-32
Copying a file from a
diskette in drive A to a
diskette in drive B

To copy a file from one disk drive to another (from drive A to B, or from drive B to A):

① Insert your DOS Tutorials diskette into one of the disk drives.

② Insert your blank formatted diskette that matches the size of the other disk drive.

③ If you are copying from drive A to B, type **COPY A:\BUSINESS.AD B:** and press **[Enter]**. If you are copying from drive B to A, type **COPY B:\BUSINESS.AD A:** and press **[Enter]**.

DOS copies the file from one disk drive to the other. If you do not specify the name of the target file for another drive, DOS assumes you want to use the same name.

Next, you want to verify the copy operations.

④ If drive B contains your target diskette, type **DIR B: /O /P** and press **[Enter]**. If drive A contains your target diskette, type **DIR A: /O /P** and press **[Enter]**. You should see BUSINESS.AD in the directory listing. See Figure 2-33.

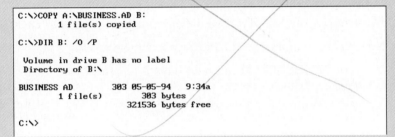

Figure 2-33
Directory listing
containing the
copied file

```
C:\>COPY A:\BUSINESS.AD B:
        1 file(s) copied

C:\>DIR B: /O /P

 Volume in drive B has no label
 Directory of B:\

BUSINESS AD          303 05-05-94   9:34a
        1 file(s)            303 bytes
                          321536 bytes free

C:\>
```

Copying a File from a Diskette to a Hard Disk, and from a Hard Disk to a Diskette

You want a copy of the business plan outline on your hard disk. If you misplaced your diskette, you will still be able to fill in the detail of the business plan.

You can copy files from a diskette to a hard disk, or vice versa (Figure 2-34). If you are completing the copy procedure in a computer lab, ask your instructor or technical support person for permission to copy to the hard disk.

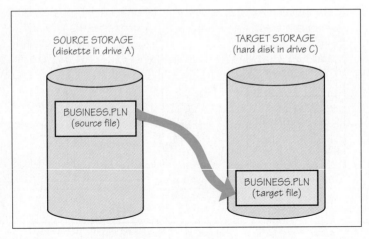

Figure 2-34
Copying a file from a
diskette in drive A to a
hard disk

To copy the business plan outline on your DOS Tutorials diskette to the hard disk:

① Type **DIR C:*.* /O /P** and press **[Enter]** to verify that the hard disk does not contain a file with the name BUSINESS.PLN in the root directory.

❷   Type **COPY A:\BUSINESS.PLN C:** and press **[Enter]**. DOS copies the file to the hard
    disk. See Figure 2-35. If you do not specify the filename of the target file, DOS uses
    the same name.

Figure 2-35
Copying a file
from a diskette
to the hard disk

```
C:\>COPY A:\BUSINESS.PLN C:\
       1 file(s) copied

C:\>
```

❸   Type **DIR C:*.* /O /P** and press **[Enter]** to verify the copy operation.

Later, after you fill in the detail for the business plan and save the changes on the hard
disk, you might want to copy the modified file to a diskette so that you have a backup copy
of the file. If you inadvertently lose the copy on the hard disk, you can use your backup
copy.

To copy from the hard disk to a diskette, you just reverse the process described above.
You specify the source drive as drive C and the target drive as either drive A or B.

Copying a File in the DOS Shell

Next, you want to copy the template for projecting your business income on a yearly basis
so that you can produce a new template for projecting income on a quarterly basis. You and
your business partner will produce new files from this template and other templates for each
job that you do. To work more efficiently, you want to learn how to use the DOS Shell to
copy files.

To copy the template file using the DOS Shell:

❶   Be sure the current drive is the drive with your DOS Tutorials diskette.

❷   Type **DOSSHELL** and press **[Enter]**.

❸   Press **[Tab]** twice to move the selection cursor to the file list window. If you are using
    the mouse, click in the file list window.

❹   Type **P** to select the first, and only, file that has the letter "P" at the beginning of its
    filename. If you are using the mouse, click in the scroll bar to the right of the file-
    names until the file PRJ_INC comes into view; then, click the filename.

❺   Press **[F10]**, press **[Enter]** to select File, and type **C** to select Copy. If you are using the
    mouse, click **File** then click **Copy**. Note that you can also use the shortcut Copy key,
    [F8]. The DOS Shell displays the Copy File dialog box. See Figure 2-36 on the follow-
    ing page. Next to the From prompt is the name of the source file. The DOS Shell will
    copy this file. Next to the To prompt, the DOS Shell displays the target drive and direc-
    tory. If you want to use another drive, you can type a new drive name. You can also
    specify a different filename for the copied file. Because this is the correct source file
    and target drive and directory, you do not need to make any changes.

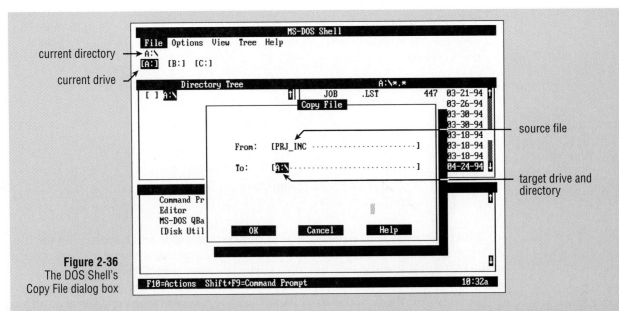

current directory
current drive

Figure 2-36
The DOS Shell's
Copy File dialog box

 ⑥   Press **[End]** to position the cursor after the drive name. If you are using the mouse, click after the drive name. If you don't press [End] or click after the drive name, the filename that you type will write over the drive name. If this happens, you will need to retype the drive name before typing the filename. Type **QTR_INC**. Then, press **[Enter]** or click **OK** with the mouse. The DOS Shell copies the file, but does not update the file list to include the new filename. You must next instruct the DOS Shell to reread your diskette.

 ⑦   Press **[F10]**, press **[→]** twice to highlight View, and press **[Enter]** to select View. Press **[↓]** six times to highlight Refresh and press **[Enter]**. If you are using the mouse, click the **View** menu, then click the **Refresh** command. Note that you can use [F5] to refresh the screen. The selection cursor returns to the drive window.

Now that you've reread your diskette, you can verify the copy operation.

 ⑧   Press **[Tab]** twice to return to the file list window. If you are using the mouse, click in the file list window. Then, type **Q** to highlight the new file QTR_INC.

 ⑨   Press **[F3]** to exit the DOS Shell.

In your business, you can quickly make copies of your template files using the DOS Shell. Then, you can modify them to produce final copies of documents for clients. Because the DOS Shell updates the directory listing with the Refresh command, you can save yourself time and effort in checking the directory before and after copy operations. This is one advantage that working in the DOS Shell has over working at the DOS prompt.

Renaming Files

You want to rename some of the files on your diskette so that the filenames more clearly identify the file contents. Later, when you are facing deadlines in your business, you will not need to spend valuable time checking to make sure you have the right file. Again, you want to compare the RENAME command at the DOS prompt with the use of the DOS Shell.

The first file that you want to rename is JOBCOSTS. You have two other JOBCOST files on your diskette that have descriptive file extensions. Because this file is a report, you want to rename it JOBCOSTS.RPT.

To rename the JOBCOSTS file from the DOS prompt:

① Be sure the current drive contains your DOS Tutorials diskette.

② Type **DIR JOBCOSTS /O /P** and press **[Enter]** to verify that the file exists.

③ Type **RENAME JOBCOSTS JOBCOSTS.RPT** and press **[Enter]**. Because you did not specify the drive name, DOS assumes you want to rename the file on the current drive. DOS will not let you rename a file if there is already a file by the name that you want to use. *You can also use the abbreviation REN instead of RENAME.*

④ Type **DIR JOBCOSTS /O /P** and press **[Enter]** to verify the change. DOS added the file extension when it renamed the file. See Figure 2-37.

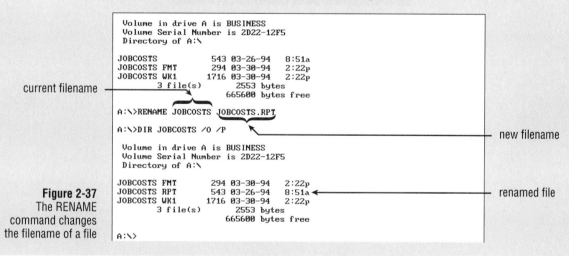

current filename

new filename

renamed file

Figure 2-37
The RENAME command changes the filename of a file

The next file that you want to rename is COVER.LTR. It is actually the letter sent with a client's resume so you want to rename it RESUME.LTR.

To rename the COVER.LTR file from the DOS Shell:

① Be sure the current drive is the drive with your DOS Tutorials diskette. Then, type **DOSSHELL** and press **[Enter]**.

② Press **[Tab]** twice to move the selection cursor to the file list window. If you are using the mouse, click in the file list window.

③ Press **[↓]** to highlight the filename COVER.LTR. If you are using the mouse, click the filename **COVER.LTR**.

④ Press **[F10]**, press **[Enter]** to select File, and type **N** to select Rename. If you are using the mouse, click **File** and then click **Rename**. The DOS Shell displays the Rename

File dialog box. See Figure 2-38. The Current name field shows the file's current name. Next to the New name prompt, you type the name you want to use.

current directory →

current drive →

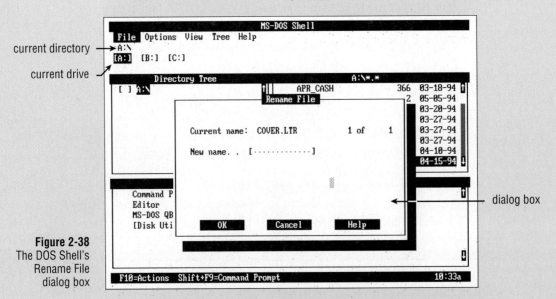

Figure 2-38
The DOS Shell's
Rename File
dialog box

dialog box

⑤   Type **RESUME.LTR**. Press **[Enter]**. If you are using the mouse, click **OK**. The DOS Shell renames the file and places it in the file list in alphabetical order.

⑥   Type **R** to display the filenames that start with the letter "R." The selection cursor is on the filename RESUME.LTR.

⑦   Press **[F3]** to exit the DOS Shell.

When you first name a file, the name you select might be logical. Later, however, you might realize that there is a better name to use for that file. You can rename it from the DOS prompt or the DOS Shell. The DOS Shell has the added advantage of quickly updating the list of filenames.

Deleting Files

You realize that you do not need a couple of the files for your business. You want to remove them from your diskette so that they do not take up valuable space. You can delete files from the DOS prompt with the DEL or ERASE commands, and from the DOS Shell. You want to compare the two different approaches.

Deleting files from the DOS prompt is somewhat risky. If you use wildcards, you can inadvertently delete important files. DOS does not ask you if you are sure you want to delete a file or a group of files except in one case. If you enter DEL *.*, DOS will automatically ask you if you want to delete all the files in the directory. As a precaution you should first test your file specification with the DIR command.

You no longer need the JOB.LST file so you decide to delete it.

To delete the file named JOB.LST at the DOS prompt:

❶ Be sure the current drive is the one with your DOS Tutorials diskette.

❷ Type **DIR JOB.LST** and press **[Enter]** to verify that the file exists. If you specify the exact name of a file, the directory listing will include only that one file.

❸ Type **DEL JOB.LST** and press **[Enter]**. *You can also use the ERASE command to achieve the same result.*

Now you want to verify the deletion.

❹ Type **DIR JOB.LST** and press **[Enter]**. The file JOB.LST is no longer on the diskette. See Figure 2-39.

```
A:\>DIR JOB.LST

 Volume in drive A is BUSINESS
 Volume Serial Number is 2D22-12F5
 Directory of A:\

JOB      LST        447 03-21-94  11:17a
         1 file(s)         447 bytes
                        665600 bytes free

A:\>DEL JOB.LST

A:\>DIR JOB.LST

 Volume in drive A is BUSINESS
 Volume Serial Number is 2D22-12F5
 Directory of A:\

File not found

A:\>
```

Figure 2-39
The DEL command
deletes a file

In the DOS Shell, you have more control over deleting files. A prompt appears on the screen asking you if you're sure you want to delete the selected file.

SCHEDULE is another file that is taking up valuable space on your diskette. You decide to use the DOS Shell to delete this file.

To delete the file named SCHEDULE using the DOS Shell:

❶ Be sure the current drive is the one with your DOS Tutorials diskette. Then, type **DOSSHELL** and press **[Enter]**.

❷ Press **[Tab]** twice until the selection cursor is in the file list window. If you are using the mouse, click in the file list window.

❸ Type **S** and note that the DOS Shell moves the cursor to the first file that starts with the letter "S" — the file you want. If you are using the mouse, click in the scroll bar to the right of the filenames until the file SCHEDULE is displayed. Then, click the filename.

❹ Press **[Del]**. The DOS Shell displays the Delete File Confirmation dialog box. See Figure 2-40 on the following page. The cursor is positioned on the Yes button. *You can also use the File Delete command to delete files. [Del] is a shortcut key.*

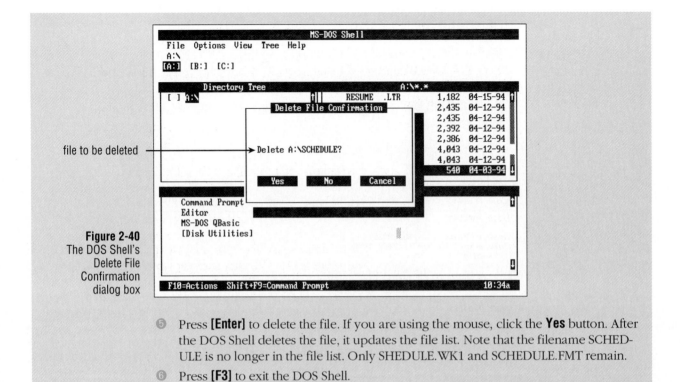

file to be deleted

Figure 2-40
The DOS Shell's
Delete File
Confirmation
dialog box

⑤ Press **[Enter]** to delete the file. If you are using the mouse, click the **Yes** button. After the DOS Shell deletes the file, it updates the file list. Note that the filename SCHEDULE is no longer in the file list. Only SHEDULE.WK1 and SCHEDULE.FMT remain.

⑥ Press **[F3]** to exit the DOS Shell.

When combined with the DIR command, the COPY, RENAME, and DEL commands assist you in one of the most important tasks you face when you use a computer system — managing your files. You can more easily and efficiently perform the same operations from the DOS Shell.

■   ■   ■

Summary

In this tutorial, you learned how to use the DIR command to display a list of the names of files stored on a diskette. You used the Pause switch to display filenames one screen at a time, the Wide switch to display filenames in columns, and the Order switch to display filenames in alphabetical order.

You created a file with the MS-DOS Editor. You explored its Help system, the Survival Guide. After entering and editing text, you used commands to save your work, to open a new file, and to exit the MS-DOS Editor. You used the TYPE command and the DOS Shell to view the contents of files. You printed copies of files with the PRINT command and the DOS Shell.

You used the COPY command to make copies of files, the RENAME command to change the name of a file, and the DEL command to delete a file from a diskette. You compared the use of these commands with the use of equivalent commands in the DOS Shell for copying, renaming, and deleting files.

Command Reference	
DOS Commands	
COPY [source] [target]	An internal command that copies a file (called the source file) and produces a new file (called the target file)
DEL [file]	An internal command that deletes a file or a group of files
DIR	An internal command that displays a directory of the diskette in the current drive, another drive, or a hard drive
DIR [file]	An internal command that displays a directory of a file on the diskette in the current drive, another drive, or a hard drive
DIR /O	An internal command that displays a directory in alphabetical order by filename and file extension
DIR /P	An internal command that displays a directory and pauses after each screen
DIR /W	An internal command that displays a directory in columns across the width of the screen, without specifying file sizes, dates, or times
DOSSHELL	An external command that loads the DOS Shell program
EDIT	An external command that loads the MS-DOS Editor into memory so you can create or work with text files
ERASE [file]	An internal command that deletes a file or a group of files
PRINT [file]	An external command that prints a text file from the DOS prompt
RENAME [file] or REN [file]	An internal command that renames a file or a group of files
TYPE [file]	An internal command that displays the contents of a text file on the screen

MS-DOS Editor Commands	
File/Exit	Exits the MS-DOS Editor
File/Open	Retrieves a file from disk
File/Save	Saves a file under the same name
File/Save As	Saves a file under a specific filename that you provide
DOS Shell Commands	
File/Copy	Copies one or more files
File/Delete	Deletes a file
File/Exit	Exits the DOS Shell
File/Print	Prints a text file from the DOS Shell, after the PRINT program is loaded from the DOS prompt
File/Rename	Renames one or more files
Options/File Display Options	Displays a file selection in the file list window
File/View File Contents	Displays the contents of a text file

Questions

Use your DOS Exercises diskette to help you answer the following questions.

1. What types of information does the DIR command provide about files stored on a diskette or hard disk?

2. What does DOS do if you enter the DIR command and do not specify a disk drive?

3. What does the Pause switch do? Give an example of how you would enter a DIR command with this switch.

4. What does the Wide switch do? Give an example of how you would enter a DIR command with this switch.

5. What does the Order switch do? Give an example of how you would enter a DIR command with this switch.

6. What function does the menu bar serve in the MS-DOS Editor and the DOS Shell? How do you access the menu bar in each?

7. What function does the title bar serve in the MS-DOS Editor?

8. What function does the status bar serve in the MS-DOS Editor?

9. What is a toggle key? Identify one toggle key covered in this tutorial.

10. What two keys can you use to edit text while using the MS-DOS Editor? How do these keys work? How do you insert text? *Cursor movement Keys + Backspace*

11. How do you save and name a file in the MS-DOS Editor?

12. Why is it important to save periodically while working on a document?

13. What is an ASCII file? What is another name for an ASCII file?

14. What DOS command can you use to display the contents of a text file? How do you use this command? *Type Filename ↵*

15. Name two ways that you can print a text file. *Print Filename ↵*

16. What is a wildcard? What wildcards can you use with DOS? Give an example of how you can use each of these wildcards.

17. What does the COPY command do? What is the difference between a source file and a target file?

18. What does DOS do when you copy a file without specifying a drive name for the source file?

19. What does DOS do when you copy a file without specifying a drive name for the target file?

20. What does DOS do when you copy a file to another disk without specifying a filename for the new file?

21. What command would you enter to display an alphabetical directory of all files that have "P" as the first character in the filename?

22. What command would you enter to display an alphabetical list of all files that have "WP" for a file extension?

23. What command would you enter to rename RESUME1, RESUME2, and RESUME3 to RESUME1.WP, RESUME2.WP, and RESUME3.WP in one step? *REN RESUME? Resume?.WP*

24. Before you delete a file what should you check?

25. Assume drive A is the current drive. What command would you enter to copy the file named 94SALES from drive A to drive C?

26. Assume drive C is the current drive. What command would you enter to delete the file named MTGNOTES on drive B? *B: Del MTGNOTES ⌐*

27. How do you view the contents of a text file in the DOS Shell?

28. How do you copy a file in the DOS Shell?

29. How do you rename a file in the DOS Shell?

30. How do you delete a file in the DOS Shell?

Tutorial Assignments

Use your DOS Exercises diskette for the following Tutorial Assignments.

1. **Displaying a Directory**: Perform the following operations from the DOS prompt. List the command that you use to accomplish each operation.
    a. Display an alphabetical directory of all files that have "I" as the first character of the filename.
    b. Display an alphabetical directory of all files that have "WK" as the first two characters of the file extension.
    c. List the total number of files on the diskette.

2. **Copying Files**: Perform the following operations from the DOS prompt. List the command you use to accomplish each operation.
    a. Copy the file named SCHEDULE and produce a new file with the name WORKLOG.
    b. Copy the file named CASHFLOW.RPT and produce a new file with the name SUMMARY.
    c. Use the ? wildcard to copy JAN_CASH, FEB_CASH, MAR_CASH, APR_CASH, MAY_CASH, and JUN_CASH to produce the files named JAN_CASH.RPT, FEB_CASH.RPT, MAR_CASH.RPT, APR_CASH.RPT, MAY_CASH.RPT, and JUN_CASH.RPT in one copy operation. *If you use the * wildcard, you might accidentally copy more files than you intended.*

3. **Viewing and Printing Text Files**: Perform the following operations from the DOS prompt. List the command that you use to accomplish each operation.
    a. Display the contents of the file named EQUIP.LST.
    b. Display the contents of the file named STARTUP.
    c. Print a copy of the file named RESUME5.DOC.

4. **Using the MS-DOS Editor**: Create a half-page document that describes three objectives you want to achieve in this course. Include the following information in the following order:
   a. Your name and date on separate lines in the upper-right corner of the document
   b. A paragraph that briefly describes why you decided to take this course
   c. A list of at least three objectives you want to achieve in this course

   Then, perform the following operations:
   d. Save your file and exit the MS-DOS Editor.
   e. Use the TYPE command to display the contents of the document.
   f. Use the PRINT command to produce a printed copy of the document.

5. **Using the DOS Shell**: Perform the following operations from the DOS Shell. List the steps for each operation, including the steps required to select a file.
   a. Copy the file JUN_CASH and produce a new file named JUL_CASH.
   b. Rename the file INVOICE.WK1 to INVOICES.WK1.
   c. Change the filename STARTUP to STARTUP.EST.
   d. Print a copy of the file RESUME1.DOC.

Tutorial 3

Using Directories

Your company, Professional Plus, is growing rapidly. You and your business partner now find that you need to more efficiently organize the files on the hard disks and diskettes in your office. You must be able to locate files more quickly and you want to make backup copies of important client and business files. If you inadvertently delete an important file or if a hard disk or diskette fails, then you can use your backup copies. Your business operations can continue without loss of income.

You will manage your files more efficiently by organizing them in directories. As your company and customer base grow, you might also need to create new directories and delete old ones. Maintaining organized files will allow you and your business partner to work more efficiently. These skills will lead you and Professional Plus to success.

OBJECTIVES

In this tutorial you will learn to:

■ Manage files

■ Print a directory

■ Create directories

■ Change directories

■ Move files to directories at the DOS prompt and the DOS Shell

■ Expand the directory structure

■ Remove directories at the DOS prompt and from the DOS Shell

■ View and print a directory tree from the DOS prompt

■ Navigate within the directory tree at the DOS prompt

■ Locate files with the DIR command at the DOS prompt and from the DOS Shell

■ Check for computer viruses

Managing Files

File management is one of the major tasks faced by any user of a computer system. This task is more complicated on a hard disk because of the enormous storage capacity of these drives. Although the hard disks in your office have 120MB of storage space, a variety of utilities and software packages, including Windows, WordPerfect, Lotus 1-2-3, and dBASE, are installed on each of the hard disks. Each software application includes hundreds of files and requires from 5 to 15MB of storage space. Already, the majority of each hard disk's storage capacity is dedicated to these software applications and utilities that you use on a daily basis. Not only must you manage the use of the files that you create with software packages, but you must also manage the files that constitute the software itself.

To assist you in this task, DOS allows you to group related files together on a hard disk or diskette. You can then work with those files as a separate unit, independent of all other files on the disk or diskette.

When you format a diskette, DOS creates a special file, called a **directory file**, to keep track of the files stored on the diskette. When you display a directory with the DIR command, DOS shows you some of the information stored in this special directory file — the name, extension, size, date, and creation or modification time of each file. This first directory created by the FORMAT command is called the **root directory**.

After you format a diskette, you can create other directories called subdirectories. A **subdirectory** is a directory that is *subordinate* to the root directory of a hard disk or diskette, or even another subdirectory. Like the root directory, subdirectories keep track of a set of files for you. Note that a subdirectory is also a directory. This tutorial will use the term *directory* to refer to a subdirectory. Remember that the term *directory* is also used to describe the output produced by the DIR command.

You can compare the use of drives, directories, and files to a filing cabinet's drawers, dividers, folders, and printed documents (Figures 3-1 and 3-2). Each drawer in a file cabinet is comparable to a disk drive. Within each drawer, each hanging folder corresponds to a directory where files are stored. For example, you might have a hanging folder named REPORTS that contains different types of organizational reports, such as sales and budget reports. Within each hanging folder, you might have folders that organize the reports by category. These folders correspond to directories below the one labeled REPORTS. You might, for example, have a folder labeled SALES that contains annual sales reports for different years. Within each folder, the individual reports correspond to a single file.

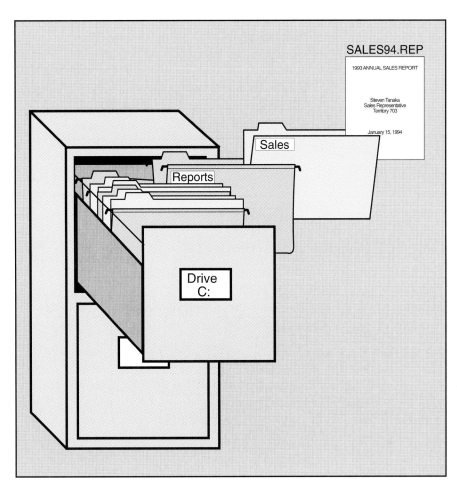

Figure 3-1
Organization of
files in directories

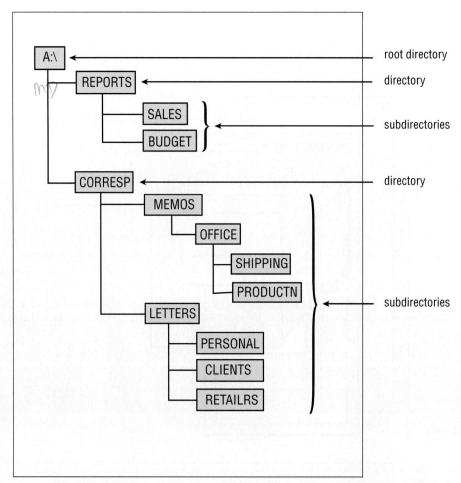

Figure 3-2
Organization of
directories and
subdirectories on a
diskette or hard disk

The organization of documents within a filing cabinet enables you to find a document quickly and easily when you need it. The same type of organization is required of a hard disk. If you organize your files by directories, store files in the appropriate directories, and maintain the directories, you can easily locate a particular file.

Before you tackle the larger task of organizing the files on your hard disk, you decide to start with the files on your diskette. Although directories are more commonly used on hard disks, you can also create directories on a diskette.

Printing a Directory

You want to start by printing a directory of all the files on your diskette so that you can plan the organization of your directories. Although DOS displays the output of the DIR command on the screen, you can **redirect**, or change the destination of, that output. You can tell DOS to send a directory listing to the printer.

Before you print a directory listing, you should install DOSKEY. Using DOSKEY can save you time and help avoid typing mistakes.

To activate DOSKEY:

1 Type **DOSKEY** and press **[Enter]**. DOS displays the message "DOSKEY installed." If you do not see this message, DOSKEY is already loaded.

Now you are ready to print a directory listing.

To print a directory listing of your DOS Tutorials diskette:

1 Be sure the current drive is the drive with your DOS Tutorials diskette.

2 Be sure the printer is on, the paper is properly aligned in the printer, and the printer is on-line.

3 Type **DIR /O>PRN** and press **[Enter]**. The symbol **>** (greater than) is called a *redirection operator;* it tells DOS to redirect the output of the DIR command to the printer. DOS prints an alphabetical directory with all the information that it would otherwise display on the screen. See Figure 3-3 on the following page. After the output is printed, you might need to eject the paper from the printer.

4 If necessary, press the Form Feed button on the printer. If the printer does not respond, press the On Line button to place the printer off-line. Then press the Form Feed button. After the printer ejects the page, press the On Line button to place the printer back on-line.

5 Remove your printed copy of the directory from the printer.

```
            Volume in drive A is BUSINESS
            Volume Serial Number is 0742-18E3
            Directory of A:\
    APR_CASH            366 03-18-94 10:20a
    BUSINESS AD         311 05-05-94 11:10a
    BUSINESS PLN        590 03-20-94  5:26p
    CASHFLOW FMT        472 03-27-94  8:32a
    CASHFLOW RPT        176 03-27-94  8:45a
    CASHFLOW WK1       1648 03-27-94  8:32a
    CLIENT   LST        476 04-10-94 11:08a
    EQUIP    LST        671 03-23-94  3:57p
    FEB_CASH            369 03-18-94 10:14a
    FEESCALE            412 04-19-94  1:48p
    INCOME   YR1        987 04-23-94  9:06a
    INCOME   YR2        987 04-23-94  9:17a
    INCOME   YR3        987 04-23-94  9:21a
    INCOME   YR4        987 04-23-94  9:34a
    INCOME   YR5        987 04-23-94  9:47a
    INSURE   LST       1528 04-09-94  8:48a
    INVOICE  FMT       2124 04-02-94 10:45a
    INVOICE  WK1       1752 04-02-94 10:45a
    INVOICES           104 03-22-94  8:48a
    JAN_CASH            368 03-18-94 10:00a
    JOBCOSTS FMT        294 03-30-94  2:22p
    JOBCOSTS RPT        543 03-26-94  8:51a
    JOBCOSTS WK1       1716 03-30-94  2:22p
    JUN_CASH            365 03-18-94 10:45a
    MAR_CASH            366 03-18-94 10:17a
    MAY_CASH            364 03-18-94 10:43a
    PRJ_INC            589 04-24-94 11:27a
    QTR_INC            589 04-24-94 11:27a
    RESUME   LTR       1182 04-15-94 11:49a
    RESUME1  DOC       2435 04-12-94  2:25p
    RESUME2  DOC       2435 04-12-94  2:41p
    RESUME3  DOC       2392 04-12-94  3:00p
    RESUME4  DOC       2386 04-12-94  3:12p
    RESUME5  DOC       4043 04-12-94  4:08p
    RESUME6  DOC       4043 04-12-94  4:08p
    SCHEDULE FMT        794 04-07-94  1:21p
    SCHEDULE WK1       2147 04-07-94  1:21P
    STARTUP           1010 03-11-94 10:03A
         38 file(s)       43995 bytes
                         667648 bytes
```

Figure 3-3
Printed directory of
the DOS Tutorials
diskette

Creating Directories

After examining the types of files on your DOS Tutorials diskette, you decide to organize the files using the directory structure shown in Figure 3-4. The DOS commands used to create a directory are **MD** and **MKDIR** (abbreviations for Make Directory).

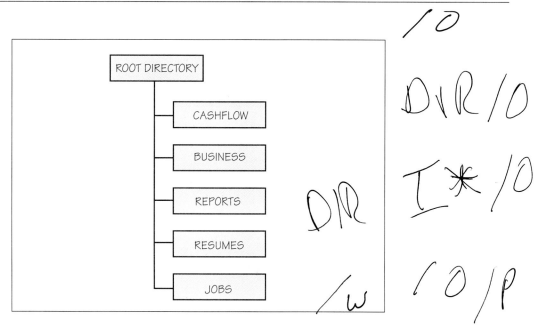

Figure 3-4
Planned directory
structure of your
DOS Tutorials
diskette

When you create a directory, you give it a name. The rules for naming a directory are the same as those for naming a file. Just as a filename identifies the type of document stored in the file, a directory's name identifies the type of files that you will store in the directory.

Before you can create a directory, check the DOS prompt to be sure you create the directory in the right place — just as you would read the label on the file drawer before placing a folder in it. You have learned that the prompt shows the current drive. It also tells you what directory you are in. For example, if you see A:\ or B:\, the letters A and B indicate the drive and the backslash (\) indicates that you are in the root directory. The backslash (\) is the notation DOS assigns to the root directory. If your DOS prompt looks like one of the examples, you are ready to create a directory.

If your DOS prompt appears as A> or B>, you need to use the PROMPT command to change the prompt so that it shows the current directory.

To change the prompt to display the current directory:

- Type **PROMPT PG** and press **[Enter]**. The *$P* tells DOS to construct the prompt so that it shows the full path name — the drive name, root directory name, and current directory name. The *$G* tells DOS to include the greater than symbol (>) after the full path name. This separates the path name from the command that you enter at the DOS prompt.

Now you are ready to create a directory.

To create the CASHFLOW directory:

- Be sure the current drive is the one with your DOS Tutorials diskette. You want the new directory on this diskette.

②   If you are using drive A, type **MD A:\CASHFLOW** and press **[Enter]**. If you are using drive B, type **MD B:\CASHFLOW** and press **[Enter]**. DOS creates the directory below the root directory of the disk drive containing your diskette, and then displays the DOS prompt again. You do not need to include the drive name in the MD command if your diskette is in the current drive but it is a good habit to develop. Including the full path forces you to think about where you want the directory to be located. Also, if you had a file with the same name you wanted to use for the directory, DOS would display an error message telling you that it is unable to create this directory. A directory name *cannot* be the same as a filename.

You want to check that you created the directory. You list all files that begin with the letter "C."

③   Type **DIR C* /O /P**. DOS displays a partial alphabetical directory listing of the files in the root directory. See Figure 3-5. The first file in the directory listing is the name of the newly created directory. DOS displays <DIR> next to each directory name in a directory listing.

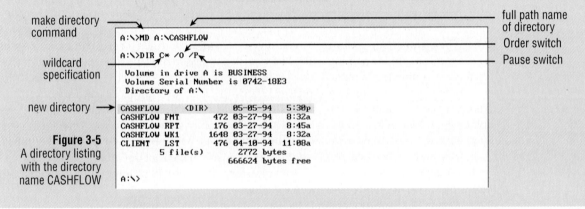

make directory command

wildcard specification

new directory →

full path name of directory
Order switch
Pause switch

Figure 3-5
A directory listing with the directory name CASHFLOW

```
A:\>MD A:\CASHFLOW

A:\>DIR C* /O /P

  Volume in drive A is BUSINESS
  Volume Serial Number is 0742-18E3
  Directory of A:\

CASHFLOW     <DIR>      05-05-94    5:30p
CASHFLOW FMT      472   03-27-94    8:32a
CASHFLOW RPT      176   03-27-94    8:45a
CASHFLOW WK1     1648   03-27-94    8:32a
CLIENT   LST      476   04-10-94   11:08a
       5 file(s)      2772 bytes
                    666624 bytes free

A:\>
```

Changing Directories

Once you create a directory, you can switch to that directory with the **CD** or **CHDIR** command (abbreviations for Change Directory). After you change to a directory, you can work with the files stored in that directory.

To change to the CASHFLOW directory:

①   Make sure the current drive is the drive with your DOS Tutorials diskette.

②   If you are using drive A, type **CD A:\CASHFLOW** and press **[Enter]**. If you are using drive B, type **CD B:\CASHFLOW** and press **[Enter]**. DOS updates the DOS prompt to show the full path name of the directory. See Figure 3-6. In this case, CASHFLOW is a directory below the root directory of the diskette in drive A (or drive B).

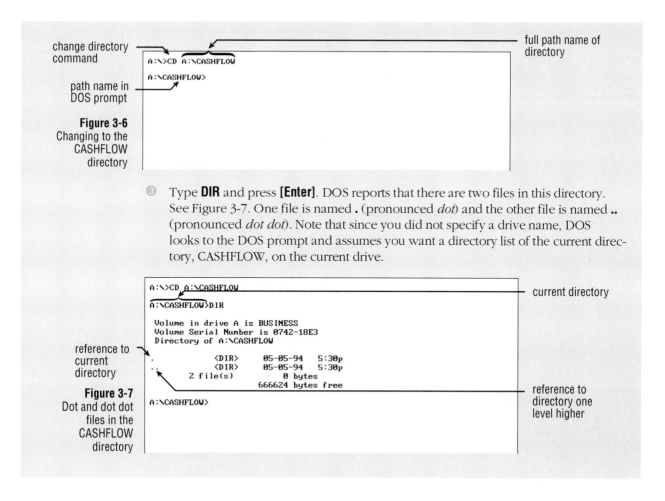

change directory command

path name in DOS prompt

full path name of directory

Figure 3-6
Changing to the
CASHFLOW
directory

③ Type **DIR** and press **[Enter]**. DOS reports that there are two files in this directory. See Figure 3-7. One file is named . (pronounced *dot*) and the other file is named .. (pronounced *dot dot*). Note that since you did not specify a drive name, DOS looks to the DOS prompt and assumes you want a directory list of the current directory, CASHFLOW, on the current drive.

current directory

reference to current directory

Figure 3-7
Dot and dot dot
files in the
CASHFLOW
directory

reference to directory one level higher

Whenever DOS creates a directory, it always creates these two files. The first file, named . (dot), is a notation for the current directory. The second file, named .. (dot dot), is a notation for the directory one level higher. In this case, it is the root directory. DOS uses the . and .. files to keep track of where it is as you move from directory to directory.

Now that you have created one of the directories planned for this diskette, you want to copy the appropriate files to this directory. You decide to return to the root directory where these files are stored.

To return to the root directory from any directory:

① Type **CD ** and press **[Enter]**. Remember, the backslash (\) is the notation assigned to the root directory. DOS updates the DOS prompt and shows the root directory as the current directory. See Figure 3-8 on the following page. If you type a slash (/) instead of a backslash (\), DOS will tell you that you have entered an invalid switch. If you type CD and do not specify a directory name, DOS will display the name of the current directory.

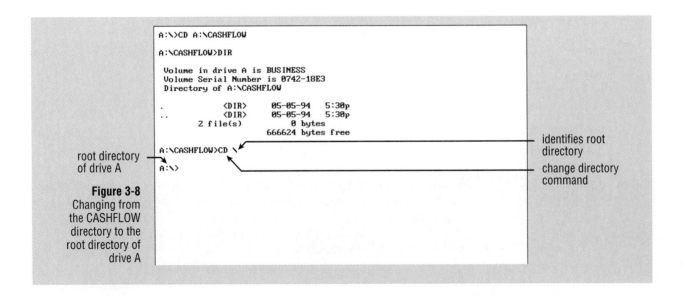

root directory
of drive A

Figure 3-8
Changing from
the CASHFLOW
directory to the
root directory of
drive A

Moving Files to a Directory at the DOS Prompt

You check your printed directory again and highlight the files that you want to move to the
CASHFLOW directory (Figure 3-9). Moving files to another directory requires two steps. First,
you copy the files to the new directory from the directory where they are currently stored.
Second, you delete the files from the original directory. It is also a good idea to verify each
of these operations with the DIR command. Because the files are similarly named, you can
use wildcards to copy them in groups, rather than one at a time. Remember, you must specify
the source file and the target file when you use the COPY command. In this case, the source
files are the files you want to copy. The target file is the CASHFLOW directory.

```
            Volume in drive A is BUSINESS
            Volume Serial Number is 1404-1821
            Directory of A:\

APR_CASH              366 03-18-94   10:20a
BUSINESS AD           303 05-05-94    2:24p
BUSINESS PLN          590 03-20-94    5:26p
CASHFLOW FMT          472 03-27-94    8:32a
CASHFLOW RPT          176 03-27-94    8:45a
CASHFLOW WK1         1648 03-27-94    8:32a
CLIENT   LST          476 04-10-94   11:08a
EQUIP    LST          671 03-23-94    3:57p
FEB_CASH              369 03-18-94   10:14a
FEESCALE              412 04-19-94    1:48p
INCOME   YR1          987 04-23-94    9:06a
INCOME   YR2          987 04-23-94    9:17a
INCOME   YR3          987 04-23-94    9:21a
INCOME   YR4          987 04-23-94    9:34a
INCOME   YR5          987 04-23-94    9:47a
INSURE   LST         1528 04-09-94    8:48a
INVOICE  FMT         2124 04-02-94   10:45a
INVOICE  WK1         1752 04-02-94   10:45a
INVOICES             104 03-22-94    8:48a
JAN_CASH             368 03-18-94   10:00a
JOBCOSTS FMT          294 03-30-94    2:22p
JOBCOSTS RPT          543 03-26-94    8:51a
JOBCOSTS WK1         1716 03-30-94    2:22p
JUN_CASH             365 03-18-94   10:45a
MAR_CASH              366 03-18-94   10:17a
MAY_CASH             364 03-18-94   10:43a
PRJ_INC              589 04-24-94   11:27a
QTR_INC              589 04-24-94   11:27a
RESUME   LTR         1182 04-15-94   11:49a
RESUME1  DOC         2435 04-12-94    2:25p
RESUME2  DOC         2435 04-12-94    2:41p
RESUME3  DOC         2392 04-12-94    3:00p
RESUME4  DOC         2386 04-12-94    3:12p
RESUME5  DOC         4043 04-12-94    4:08p
RESUME6  DOC         4043 04-12-94    4:08p
SCHEDULE FMT          794 04-07-94    1:21p
SCHEDULE WK1         2147 04-07-94    1:21p
STARTUP             1010 03-11-94   10:03a
        38 file(s)        43987 bytes
                         667648 bytes free
```

Figure 3-9
Selection of files
for the CASHFLOW
directory

To copy the files to the CASHFLOW directory:

① Be sure the current drive contains your DOS Tutorials diskette.

② If you are using drive A, type **COPY A:\CASH*.* A:\CASHFLOW** and press **[Enter]**. If you are using drive B, substitute the drive name B: for A:. DOS copies three files —

CASHFLOW.FMT, CASHFLOW.WK1, and CASHFLOW.RPT to the new directory. If the current drive is the one with your DOS Tutorials diskette, you do not need to specify the drive name.

    ③ Type **DIR A:\CASHFLOW /O /P** and press **[Enter]**. The three copied files are stored in the CASHFLOW directory. See Figure 3-10.

source files ——————

target directory ——————

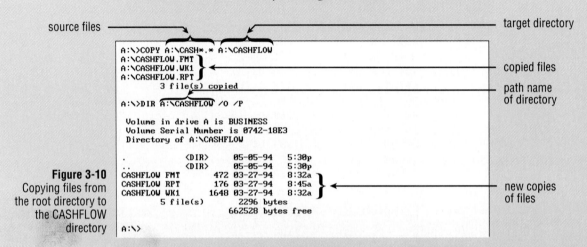

Figure 3-10
Copying files from
the root directory to
the CASHFLOW
directory

copied files

path name
of directory

new copies
of files

    ④ Type **COPY A:\INCOME.* A:\CASHFLOW** and press **[Enter]**. DOS copies five files — INCOME.YR5, INCOME.YR1, INCOME.YR4, INCOME.YR2, and INCOME.YR3.

    ⑤ Type **COPY A:\???_INC A:\CASHFLOW** and press **[Enter]**. DOS copies PRJ_INC and QTR_INC to the CASHFLOW directory.

    ⑥ Type **DIR CASHFLOW /O /P** and press **[Enter]** to verify the copy operations. Figure 3-11 shows the files that you copied to the CASHFLOW directory.

directory name ——————

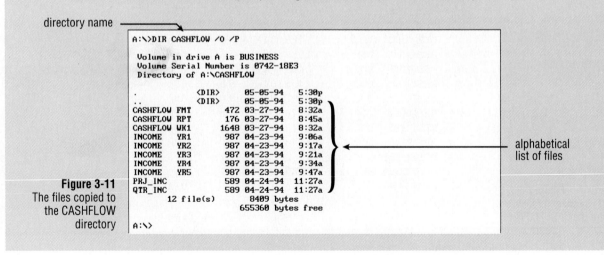

Figure 3-11
The files copied to
the CASHFLOW
directory

alphabetical
list of files

You now have two copies of the files on the same diskette. One copy is in the CASHFLOW directory and one copy is in the root directory. This is not an efficient use of disk space. You need to delete the original copies of the files in the root directory.

To delete the original files in the root directory:

❶ Be sure you are at the root directory of the drive containing your DOS Tutorials diskette (A:\> or B:\>).

❷ Type **DEL A:\CASH*.*** and press **[Enter]**. DOS deletes these files. If the current drive is the one with your diskette, you do not need to specify the drive name.

❸ Type **DEL INCOME.*** and press **[Enter]**.

❹ Type **DEL ???_INC** and press **[Enter]**.

❺ Type **DIR /O /P** and press **[Enter]** to verify the deletions. The files that you copied are no longer in the root directory.

❻ Type **CD A:\CASHFLOW** and press **[Enter]** to change to the CASHFLOW directory.

❼ Type **DIR /O /P** and press **[Enter]**. This directory still contains the copies of the files. The DEL command deleted the files from the root directory, but not from the new directory. The DOS directory structure enables you to perform operations within a directory without affecting another directory.

After examining the CASHFLOW directory, you realize that three other files belong in this directory. These files begin with the word "INVOICE." You decide to copy them from the root directory to the directory that you are currently in. The source files are the files in the root directory that you want to copy, and the target file is the current directory.

To copy the INVOICE files from the root directory to the current directory:

❶ If you are using drive A, type **COPY A:\INVOICE*.*** and press **[Enter]**. If you are using drive B, substitute the drive name B: for A:. DOS copies three files — INVOICE.WK1, INVOICES, and INVOICE.FMT. Because you did not specify the target directory, DOS assumes you want to use the current directory.

❷ Type **DIR /O /P** and press **[Enter]** to verify the copy operation. The three files are stored in the CASHFLOW directory. You can now delete them from the root directory.

❸ Type **DEL A:\INVOICE*.*** and press **[Enter]**. *If you do not specify the full path, you will delete the files from the CASHFLOW directory.* If you inadvertently delete the files from this directory, you will have to copy them from the root directory again.

❹ Type **DIR A:\INVOICE*.*** and press **[Enter]**. DOS tells you that the file was not found. DOS deleted the files from the root directory.

You and your business partner want to project expected income and expenses so that you can anticipate cash needs. You also want to keep a record of your actual income and expenses so that you can compare this information later with your initial projections. As your projections more closely match your actual cash flow, you and your business partner will be able to operate your business successfully.

Your new directory already contains files that you will use to project income and expenses. To save time and effort you decide to copy these files so that you can modify them later to track actual income and expenses. Since you will use these two sets of files in conjunction with each other, you decide to store them in the same directory.

To copy the cashflow files within the CASHFLOW directory:

1. Be sure you are in the CASHFLOW directory. The DOS prompt should contain the word CASHFLOW.

2. Type **COPY CASHFLOW.* CASH.*** and press **[Enter]**. DOS copies three files.

3. Type **DIR CASH* /O /P** and press **[Enter]** to view the new files. Now there are six files that begin with CASH in the CASHFLOW directory.

4. Type **CD ** and press **[Enter]** to return to the root directory.

Now, you need to create a directory for your general business files. These files include the ones with your business plan, business advertisement, estimated startup costs, and checklists for starting this business.

To create the BUSINESS directory:

1. Be sure you are at the root directory of your DOS Tutorials diskette (A:\> or B:\>).

2. Type **MD BUSINESS** and press **[Enter]**. DOS creates the directory and displays the DOS prompt. You could also enter MD A:\BUSINESS (or MD B:\BUSINESS) to create the directory. If you do not specify the drive or the current directory, DOS checks the DOS prompt for this information. In this case, the current drive is drive A (or drive B) and the current directory is the root directory. DOS then creates the directory below the root directory on drive A (or drive B). You can save yourself time and keystroking when you work at the DOS prompt by letting DOS locate this information for you.

Now, you are ready to copy the files to this new directory.

3. Type **COPY BUSINESS.* BUSINESS** and press **[Enter]**. DOS copies BUSINESS.PLN and BUSINESS.AD to the BUSINESS directory. Be sure DOS displays these file-names before you delete them in the next step.

4. Type **DEL BUSINESS.*** and press **[Enter]** to delete the files from the root directory.

5. Type **COPY STARTUP BUSINESS** and press **[Enter]** to copy the file to the BUSINESS directory.

6. Type **DEL STARTUP** and press **[Enter]** to delete the file from the root directory.

7. Type **COPY *.LST BUSINESS** and press **[Enter]**. DOS copies CLIENT.LST, EQUIP.LST, and INSURE.LST to the BUSINESS directory.

8. **Type DEL *.LST** and press **[Enter]** to delete the files from the root directory.

9. Type **CD BUSINESS** and press **[Enter]** to change to the BUSINESS directory.

10. With DOSKEY installed, recall the DIR/O/P command with **[↑]**. Otherwise, type **DIR /O /P** and press **[Enter]**. The BUSINESS directory contains the six files that you copied to it. See Figure 3-12.

change directory command

current directory

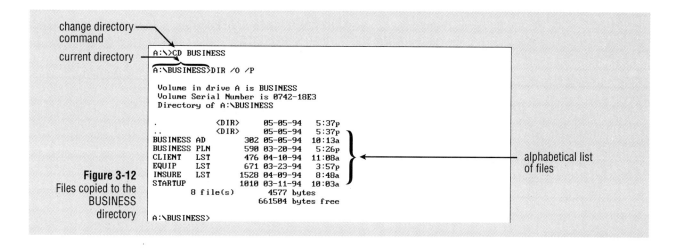

```
A:\>CD BUSINESS

A:\BUSINESS>DIR /O /P

 Volume in drive A is BUSINESS
 Volume Serial Number is 0742-18E3
 Directory of A:\BUSINESS

.               <DIR>       05-05-94    5:37p
..              <DIR>       05-05-94    5:37p
BUSINESS AD          302 05-05-94   10:13a
BUSINESS PLN         590 03-20-94    5:26p
CLIENT   LST         476 04-10-94   11:08a
EQUIP    LST         671 03-23-94    3:57p
INSURE   LST        1528 04-09-94    8:40a
STARTUP             1010 03-11-94   10:03a
        8 file(s)          4577 bytes
                         661504 bytes free

A:\BUSINESS>
```

alphabetical list of files

Figure 3-12
Files copied to the BUSINESS directory

Finally, you want a directory for your monthly cash flow reports. You want to name this directory REPORTS and you want to create it below the root directory. Although you are still working in the BUSINESS directory, you can create this new directory if you provide DOS with its full path name — A:\REPORTS (or B:\REPORTS). You must specify the name of the root directory so that DOS creates this new directory below the root directory of drive A (or drive B). If you only specify the directory name REPORTS, DOS will create the new directory below the BUSINESS directory instead (Figure 3-13). It is important to specify enough of the path name so that DOS places the directory in the correct location.

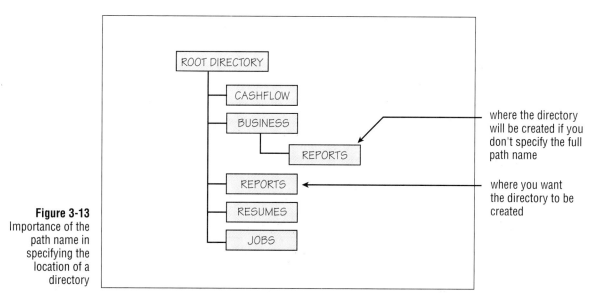

where the directory will be created if you don't specify the full path name

where you want the directory to be created

Figure 3-13
Importance of the path name in specifying the location of a directory

To create the REPORTS directory:

❶ If you are using drive A, type **MD A:\REPORTS** and press **[Enter]**. If you are using drive B, type **MD B:\REPORTS** and press **[Enter]**. Now, you can copy files from the root directory to this new directory. Again, you must specify its full path name as the target directory.

② If you are using drive A, type **COPY A:\???_CASH A:\REPORTS** and press **[Enter]**. If you are using drive B, type **COPY B:\???_CASH B:\REPORTS** and press **[Enter]**. DOS copies APR_CASH, MAY_CASH, MAR_CASH, FEB_CASH, JUN_CASH, and JAN_CASH to the REPORTS directory. You must specify the name of the root directory for the source files so that DOS knows where the files are located. You must also inform DOS that the target directory is below the root directory; otherwise, DOS will assume it is below the current directory. If you did not specify the exact location of the target directory, DOS would copy all the files into one file named "REPORTS" in the current directory.

③ If you are using drive A, type **DIR A:\REPORTS /O /P** and press **[Enter]**. If you are using drive B, type **DIR B:\REPORTS /O /P** and press **[Enter]**. This operation verifies that the files are stored in the REPORTS directory before you delete them from the root directory. See Figure 3-14.

current directory ────────→   full path name of directory

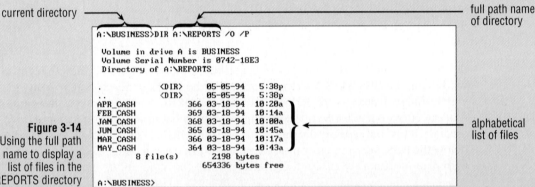

Figure 3-14
Using the full path name to display a list of files in the REPORTS directory

alphabetical list of files

④ If you are using drive A, type **DEL A:\???_CASH** and press **[Enter]**. If you are using drive B, type **DEL B:\???_CASH** and press **[Enter]**. DOS deletes the files from the root directory.

⑤ If you are using drive A, type **CD A:\REPORTS** and press **[Enter]**. If you are using drive B, type **CD B:\REPORTS** and press **[Enter]**. DOS changes to the new directory from another directory at the same level.

⑥ Use **[↑]** to recall the DIR/O/P command or type **DIR /O /P** and press **[Enter]** to verify that you did not delete the files you copied to this directory. The six files are still in this directory because you specified the full path name during the delete operation. See Figure 3-15.

current directory ────────→   change directory command

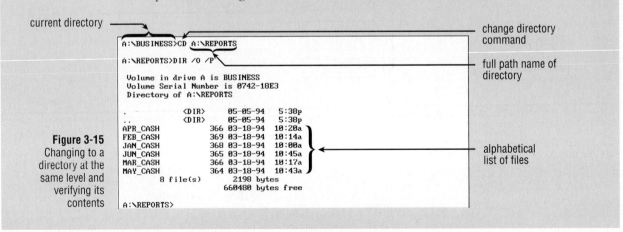

Figure 3-15
Changing to a directory at the same level and verifying its contents

full path name of directory

alphabetical list of files

⑦ Type **CD ** and press **[Enter]** to return to the root directory.

Moving Files to a Directory from the DOS Shell

You decide to create the remaining directories from the DOS Shell. As you have discovered, the DOS Shell provides a visual interface, automatically displays directories and filenames, and simplifies DOS command operations. You can use the DOS Shell to move files from one directory to another. Because the DOS Shell can move files in one step, you can more quickly reorganize your DOS Tutorials diskette and verify the changes that you make.

To load the DOS Shell:

① Be sure you are at the root directory. If not, type **CD ** and press **[Enter]**.

② Type **DOSSHELL** and press **[Enter]**. After DOS loads the DOS Shell, note that the Directory Tree window contains a diagram showing the directory structure of the diskette. See Figure 3-16.

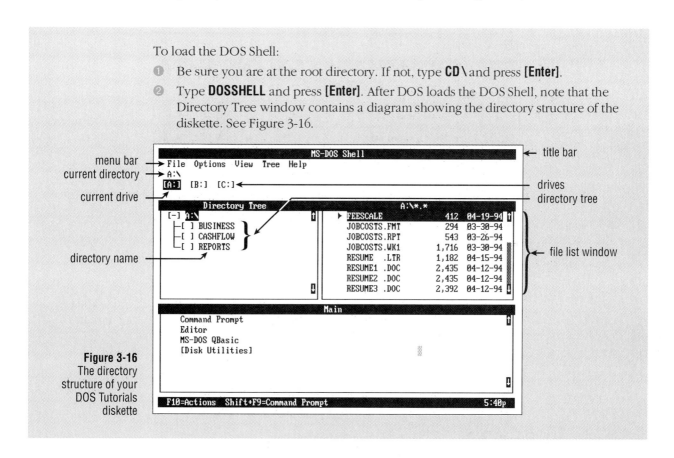

Figure 3-16
The directory structure of your DOS Tutorials diskette

This diagram is called a **directory tree**; it shows the relationship of directories to the root directory. The A:\ in the Directory Tree window is highlighted, indicating that it is the current directory. If your DOS Tutorials diskette is in drive B, then you will see B:\ in this window. The directory tree shows the three directories that you created earlier at the DOS prompt.

In the file list window, the DOS Shell shows the files stored in the root directory because that directory is the current directory. In the title bar for the file list window, the DOS Shell displays **A:*.*** to indicate that the file list contains all files in the root directory of drive A.

You need to create two more directories according to your revised plan — RESUMES and JOBS.

To create a directory from the DOS Shell:

1. Press **[Tab]** to move to the Directory Tree window. If you are using the mouse, click the root directory in the Directory Tree window.

2. Press **[F10]** to access the menu bar, press **[Enter]** to select the File menu, then type **E** to select the Create Directory command. If you are using the mouse, click **File** then click **Create Directory**. The DOS Shell displays the Create Directory dialog box. See Figure 3-17. The dialog box shows the parent name, in this case, A:\, and prompts for the new directory name. A *parent directory* is a directory that contains one or more directories below it.

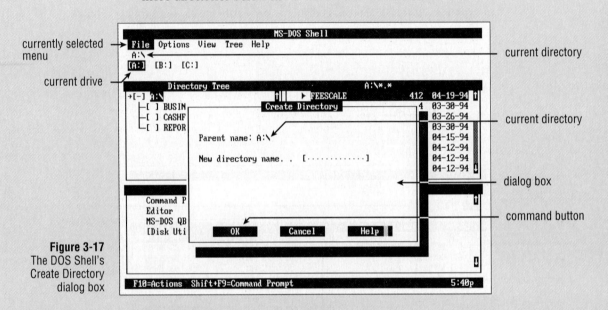

currently selected menu

current drive

current directory

current directory

dialog box

command button

Figure 3-17
The DOS Shell's
Create Directory
dialog box

3. Type **RESUMES**. Then, press **[Enter]**. If you are using the mouse, click **OK**. The DOS Shell creates the RESUMES directory on the current drive, drive A, then updates the directory tree. See Figure 3-18.

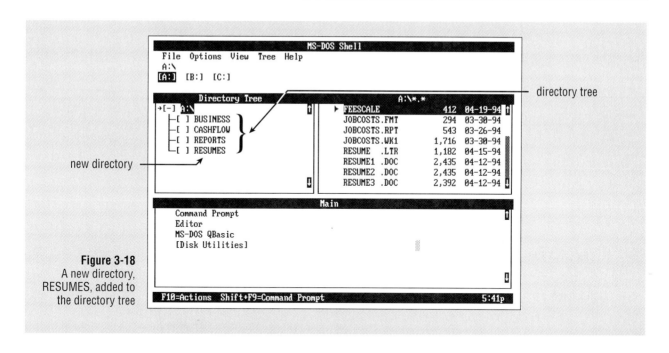

directory tree

new directory

Figure 3-18
A new directory,
RESUMES, added to
the directory tree

Now, you must select the files to move to the RESUMES directory. Instead of moving the files one at a time, you can move them as a group in one step. You do not need to copy the files to a new directory and then delete them from the original directory where they are stored.

To move the resume template files from the root directory to the RESUMES directory:

① Press **[Tab]**. The DOS Shell moves the selection cursor to the file list window. If you are using the mouse, click in the file list window.

② Type **R** to move the selection cursor to the first file that starts with the letter "R." If you are using the mouse, click the filename **RESUME.LTR**. The DOS Shell highlights the filename RESUME.LTR.

③ Press and hold down **[Shift]** while you press **[↓]** six times to highlight the files with RESUME as the first six characters of the filename. The last filename in this group is RESUME6.DOC. Then, release **[Shift]**. If you are using the mouse, first click the down arrow on the vertical scroll bar to the left of the filenames so that you can see the filename RESUME6.DOC. Press and hold down **[Shift]** while you click the filename **RESUME6.DOC**. Then release **[Shift]**. Figure 3-19 on the following page shows the selected files.

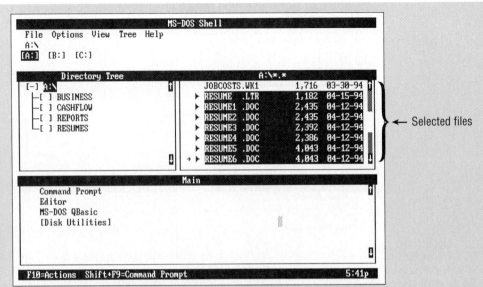

Figure 3-19
Selecting a group of
files to move to the
RESUMES directory

4. If you are using the keyboard, press **[F10]**, then press **[Enter]** to select the File menu. Type **M** to select the Move command. The DOS Shell displays the Move File dialog box. See Figure 3-20. The selected files are listed in the first text box, next to the From prompt. You can see only a partial list of files in this text box. The cursor is in the next text box, to the right of the To prompt. The DOS Shell assumes you want to move the files to the current directory. Press **[End]** to move the cursor past the full path name of the current directory. Then, type **RESUMES** to specify the full path name of the new directory, and press **[Enter]**. The DOS Shell moves the seven files to the RESUMES directory.

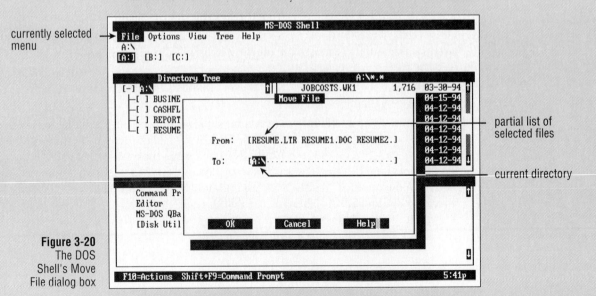

Figure 3-20
The DOS
Shell's Move
File dialog box

If you are using the mouse, click one of the selected files, hold down the mouse button and drag the pointer to the directory named RESUMES in the Directory Tree window. As you point to this directory, the pointer changes to an arrow if you are in text mode or a stack of documents or files if you are in graphics mode. Then, release the mouse button. The DOS Shell displays the Confirm Mouse Operation dialog box and asks if you want to move the selected files to A:\RESUMES. Click **Yes**. The DOS Shell moves the files to the RESUMES directory.

Next, you want to verify these operations and be sure your business files are stored in the current directory. First, you must use [F5] so that the DOS Shell rereads your diskette and refreshes the display of files on your DOS Tutorials diskette.

To refresh the display of the files on your DOS Tutorials diskette:

① Press **[F5]** to refresh the display of the files. If you are using the mouse, click **View** and **Refresh**.

② Press **[Tab]** to move to the Directory Tree window. Then, press [↓] four times. If you are using the mouse, click each directory name. The DOS Shell updates the file list window to show the files in the selected directory. RESUMES contains the seven files that you just moved. See Figure 3-21.

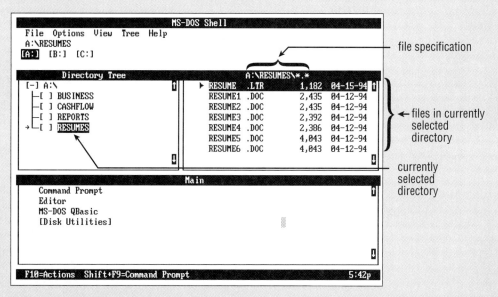

Figure 3-21
Verifying the contents of the RESUMES directory

③ Press **[Home]** to move the selection cursor to the root directory. If you are using the mouse, click the root directory.

According to your organizational plan, you have one more directory to create. This directory, named JOBS, will contain the files that store information on each job that you do for a client.

To create the JOBS directory:

① Create the JOBS directory according to your original plan for organizing directories and files on your DOS Tutorials diskette.

② After you create the JOBS directory, move the remaining files to this directory. Move the cursor to the Directory Tree window and highlight the JOBS directory. The DOS Shell updates the file list window to show the files in the JOBS directory. See Figure 3-22.

current directory →

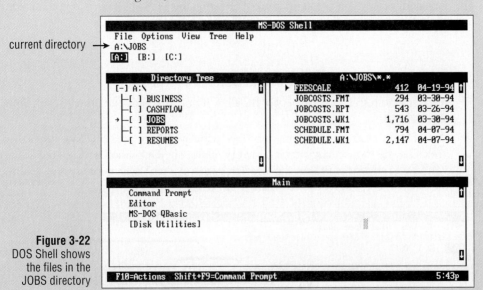

Figure 3-22
DOS Shell shows
the files in the
JOBS directory

③ Press **[F5]** to refresh the display of files on your diskette. If you are using the mouse, click **View** and **Refresh**.

You have created five directories and moved groups of files to those directories using both the DOS prompt and the DOS Shell. Because your DOS Tutorials diskette has changed significantly, you might want to make a backup copy of it. If you would like to make a backup copy, use the DISKCOPY command and refer to page DOS 27 for help.

If you need to take a break, be sure to remove all diskettes from the computer before leaving. If you're working in a lab, ask your instructor or technical support person whether it is necessary to turn off the computer. If so, locate the power switch and turn it to the "OFF" position. Then, locate the power switch to the monitor and turn off the power. If you want to continue working, go on to the next section.

Expanding the Directory Structure

After reorganizing the files on your diskette into directories, you realize that you could create several directories below the CASHFLOW directory and organize the files into smaller groups. Then, you would be able to work more easily with the files. You can also add more files to each directory as the need arises. Figure 3-23 shows your updated plan for organizing the CASHFLOW directory into three directories — one called "PRJCASH" for storing cash flow projections for your business, one called "INVOICES" for storing files used to track the status of outstanding invoices, and one called "SUMMARY" for summary report files.

The first directory you will create is PRJCASH. This directory will contain the five INCOME files along with PRJ_INC and QTR_INC.

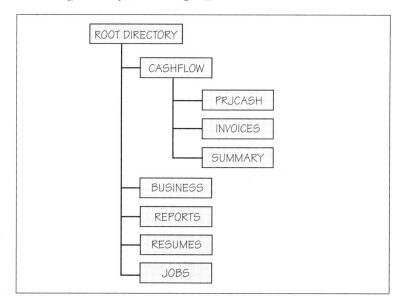

Figure 3-23
Revised directory
structure of your
DOS Tutorials
diskette

To create the PRJCASH directory below the CASHFLOW directory:

① Be sure the selection cursor is on the root directory in the Directory Tree window.

② Press [↓] twice to highlight the directory name CASHFLOW. If you are using the mouse, click the directory name **CASHFLOW** in the Directory Tree window. The DOS Shell selects this directory and updates the file list window.

③ Press **[F10]** to access the menu bar, press **[Enter]** to select the File menu, and then type **E** to select the Create Directory command. If you are using the mouse, click **File** then click **Create Directory**. The DOS Shell displays the Create Directory dialog box. The parent directory's full path name is A:\CASHFLOW (or B:\CASHFLOW).

④ Type **PRJCASH**. Then press **[Enter]**. If you are using the mouse, click **OK**. The DOS Shell creates the PRJCASH directory below the current directory. See Figure 3-24 on the following page.

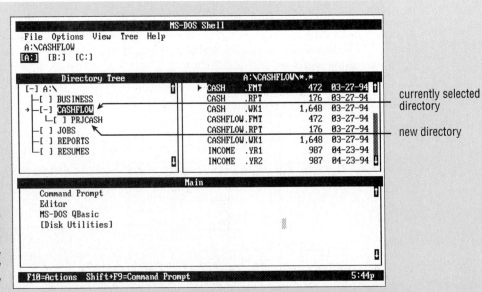

Figure 3-24
The newly added
PRJCASH
directory below
the CASHFLOW
directory

⑤   Press **[Tab]** to move to the file list window. If you are using the mouse, click in this window.

Now you are ready to select the files to move.

⑥   Type **I** to move the selection cursor to the filename INCOME.YR1. If you are using the mouse, click the filename **INCOME.YR1**.

⑦   Press and hold down **[Shift]** while you press **[↓]** four times to select the next four files — INCOME.YR2, INCOME.YR3, INCOME.YR4, and INCOME.YR5.

If you are using the mouse, click the down arrow on the vertical scroll bar until you see the filename INCOME.YR5. Then press and hold down **[Shift]**, click the filename **INCOME.YR5**, and release **[Shift]**. You need to add two more files to your selection but they do not follow the files you just highlighted.

⑧   To add more files to this selection, press and hold down **[Shift]** while you press **[F8]**. Then release both **[F8]** and **[Shift]**. The ADD indicator appears in the lower-right corner of the screen next to the time. Type **P** to move the selection cursor to the file PRJ_INC. Press **[Space]** to add this file to the selection. Press **[↓]** to highlight QTR_INC. Finally, press **[Space]** to add this file to the selection.

If you are using the mouse, click in the scroll bar until you see the filename QTR_INC. Press and hold **[Ctrl]** while you click **PRJ_INC** and then **QTR_INC**. Release **[Ctrl]**. Figure 3-25 shows part of the selected files.

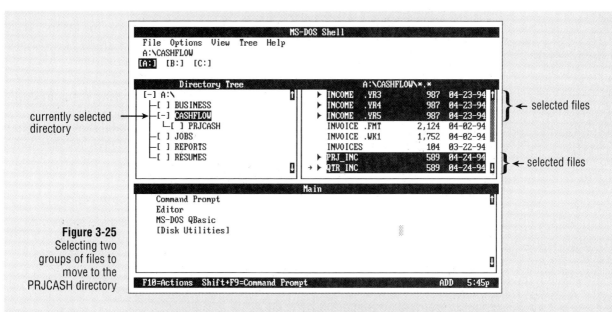

Figure 3-25
Selecting two
groups of files to
move to the
PRJCASH directory

⑨   Press **[F7]**. The DOS Shell displays the Move File dialog box with the path name
    A:\CASHFLOW (or B:\CASHFLOW). Press **[End]** and type **\PRJCASH**. You *must*
    type the backslash (\) before PRJCASH to separate the name of this directory from
    its parent directory name. See Figure 3-26 to be sure you enter the path correctly.
    Then, press **[Enter]**. The DOS Shell moves the files to the PRJCASH directory.

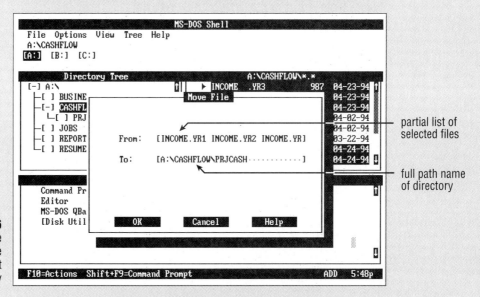

Figure 3-26
Specifying the
full path name
of the target
directory

    If you are using the mouse, click one of the selected files, hold down the mouse
    button and drag the pointer to the directory named **PRJCASH** in the Directory
    Tree window. Then, release the left mouse button. The DOS Shell displays the
    Confirm Mouse Operation dialog box and asks if you want to move the files to
    A:\CASHFLOW\PRJCASH. Click **Yes**. The DOS Shell moves the files to the
    PRJCASH directory.

    Next, you want to verify these operations before you make any more directories.

⑩ Press **[F5]** to refresh the display of files on your diskette. If you are using the mouse, click **View** and **Refresh**.

After you tell the DOS Shell to refresh the display of files on a diskette, it automatically collapses the directory tree so that you see only the directories below the root directory. You do not see the directories below the CASHFLOW directory. However, the DOS Shell places a plus sign (+) next to the directory name CASHFLOW to indicate that there are directories below it.

To view the directories as part of the directory tree, you must next expand the directory tree:

① Press **[F10]**, press **[→]** three times to highlight the Tree menu, and press **[Enter]** to select Tree. If you are using the mouse, click **Tree**. The drop-down Tree menu appears with options for controlling the display of the directory tree.

② Press **[↓]** twice to highlight Expand All, then press **[Enter]** to select this option. If you are using the mouse, click **Expand All**. The DOS Shell expands the directory tree. Now you can view the files in each of the directories below the CASHFLOW directory.

③ Press **[Tab]** to move to the Directory Tree window. Then press **[↓]** three times to highlight the directory name PRJCASH. If you are using the mouse, click the directory name **PRJCASH**. The file list window displays the files that you moved to the PRJCASH directory. See Figure 3-27. Note the full path name in the title bar of the file list window.

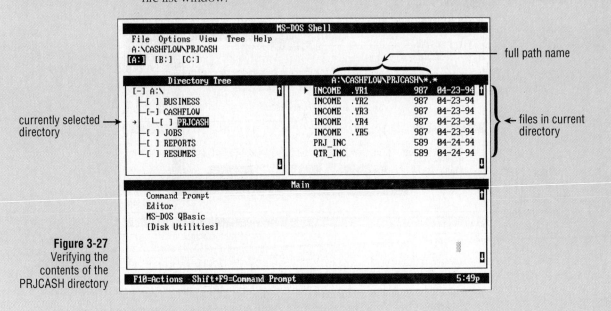

Figure 3-27
Verifying the contents of the PRJCASH directory

Since a new business must stay on top of its cash flow, you want to be able to quickly examine the status of outstanding invoices. You decide to create a new directory below the CASHFLOW directory and move the invoice-tracking files to that directory.

To create the INVOICES directory:

① Press [↑] to select the CASHFLOW directory. If you are using the mouse, click the directory name **CASHFLOW**.

② Press **[F10]** to access the menu bar, press **[Enter]** to select the File menu, and then type **E** to select the Create Directory command. If you are using the mouse, click **File** and then click **Create Directory**.

③ Type **INVOICES**. Then press **[Enter]**. If you are using the mouse, click **OK**. The DOS Shell displays the Create Directory dialog box and displays the message "Access denied." See Figure 3-28. The dialog box asks you to verify whether or not you want to continue. An error has occurred. The directory name that you specified is also the name of an existing file. You have two options — rename the file or choose to call the directory something else.

④ You decide to rename the file. Press **[Enter]** to skip this file or directory and continue, or click **OK** with the mouse.

Figure 3-28
The DOS Shell's
Create Directory
dialog box warns of
an error

⑤ Press **[Tab]** to move to the file list window. If you are using the mouse, click in the file list window.

⑥ Type **I** to select the first filename that starts with the letter "I." Then press [↓] twice to highlight the filename INVOICES. If you are using the mouse, click the scroll arrow until you see the filename INVOICES, then click **INVOICES**.

⑦ Press **[F10]**, press **[Enter]** to select File, and type **N** for the Rename command. If you are using the mouse, click **File** then click **Rename**. When the Rename File dialog box appears, type **INVOICE.RPT** for the new filename and press **[Enter]**. The DOS Shell renames the file and updates the file list window.

⑧ Press **[Shift] [Tab]**. This returns you to the Directory Tree window. This key combination is called the *backtab key* because it allows you to move back to the previous window. If you are using the mouse, click the **CASHFLOW** directory in the Directory Tree window.

⑨ Be sure the DOS Shell highlights the directory name CASHFLOW.

Now that you have renamed the INVOICES file, you can create the INVOICES directory.

To create the INVOICES directory:

① Press **[F10]** to access the menu bar, press **[Enter]** to select the File menu, and then type **E** to select the Create Directory command. If you are using the mouse, click **File** then click **Create Directory**. Type **INVOICES**. Then press **[Enter]**. If you are using the mouse, click **OK**. The DOS Shell adds the INVOICES directory to the directory tree, below CASHFLOW.

② Press **[Tab]** to move to the file list window. If you are using the mouse, click in the file list window.

③ Type **I** to select the first filename that starts with the letter "I." If you are using the mouse, click the scroll arrow until you see the first filename that starts with the letter "I." Then click the filename.

④ Press and hold **[Shift]** while you press **[↓]** twice to select the three invoice files. Release **[Shift]**. If you are using the mouse, press **[Shift]** and then click the filename **INVOICE.WK1** to select the three invoice files.

⑤ Press **[F7]**. The DOS Shell displays the Move File dialog box. Press **[End]**, type **\INVOICES**, and press **[Enter]**. If you are using the mouse, click **File** then click **Move**. When the DOS Shell displays the Move File dialog box, click after the path name. Then type **\INVOICES** and click **OK**. The DOS Shell moves the files to the INVOICES directory.

⑥ Press **[F5]** to refresh the display of files on your diskette. If you are using the mouse, click **View** then click **Refresh**.

⑦ Press **[F10]**, press **[→]** three times to highlight Tree, and press **[Enter]** to select Tree. If you are using the mouse, click **Tree**.

⑧ Press **[↓]** twice to highlight Expand All. Then press **[Enter]**. If you are using the mouse, click **Expand All**. The DOS Shell expands the directory tree.

You have one more directory to create according to your revised plan. This directory, the SUMMARY directory, will store the files that contain the cash flow summaries.

To create the SUMMARY directory:

① Create the SUMMARY directory according to your revised plan for organizing directories and files on your diskette.

➋ After you create the SUMMARY directory, move the remaining files to this directory. No files remain in the CASHFLOW directory. Refresh your screen view. Move to the Directory Tree window and highlight the SUMMARY directory. The DOS Shell updates the file list window to show the files in the SUMMARY directory. See Figure 3-29.

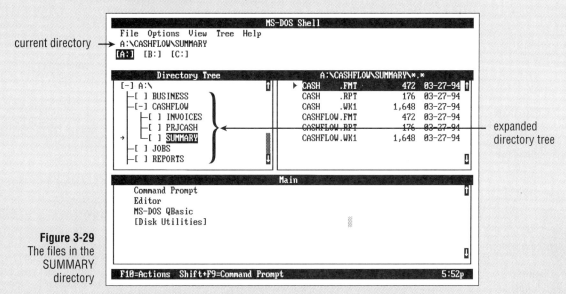

Figure 3-29
The files in the SUMMARY directory

➌ Press **[Home]** to return to the root directory. If you are using the mouse, click the root directory name.

➍ Press **[F3]** to exit the DOS Shell.

Removing Directories

You meet with your business partner to discuss the new organization of the diskette. Your business partner decides to maintain the files that contain the monthly cash flow reports and the cash flow summaries. Because these files are on your partner's hard drive, you do not need to keep them on your diskette. If you remove these files and the two directories where these files are stored, you can free more space on your diskette. These two directories are named REPORTS and CASHFLOW\SUMMARY.

Removing a directory requires two steps. First, you must move or delete all the files in the directory. Second, you remove the empty directory with the **RD** or **RMDIR** command (abbreviations for Remove Directory). You *cannot* remove a directory that you are currently in; that is, you *must* first change to another directory. Also, you cannot remove a directory if it contains directories below it.

First, you will delete the files in the REPORTS directory. The DEL command does not remove a directory. However, you can use the DEL command to delete all of the files in a directory.

To remove the REPORTS directory:

❶ Be sure the current drive is the one with your DOS Tutorials diskette. Also, be sure you are at the root directory. If not, type **CD ** and press **[Enter]**.

❷ Use the [↑] key to recall the DIR/O/P command or type **DIR /O /P** and press **[Enter]**. DOS shows you the five directories below the root directory. See Figure 3-30.

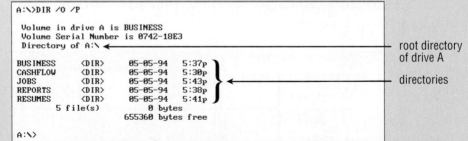

Figure 3-30
Displaying the directories below the root directory

root directory of drive A

directories

❸ Type **DEL REPORTS** and press **[Enter]**. DOS warns you that it will delete all the files in the directory. See Figure 3-31. In response to the prompt, "Are you sure (Y/N)?", type **Y** for Yes and press **[Enter]**. Now, you can remove the directory.

delete command

Figure 3-31
DOS prompts for verification before deleting all the files in a directory

directory name
prompt for verification

❹ Type **RD REPORTS** and press **[Enter]**. DOS removes this empty directory.

❺ Use [↑] to recall the DIR/O/P command or type **DIR /O /P** and press **[Enter]** to verify that DOS has removed the REPORTS directory. See Figure 3-32.

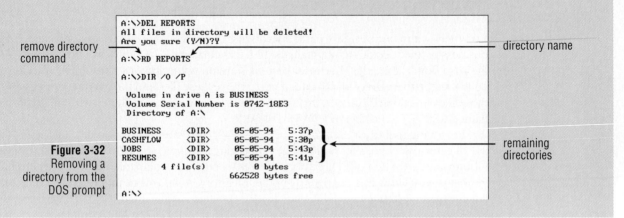

remove directory command

directory name

Figure 3-32
Removing a directory from the DOS prompt

remaining directories

You want to remove the other directory, CASHFLOW\SUMMARY, using the DOS Shell.

To remove the CASHFLOW\SUMMARY directory using the DOS Shell:

① Use **[↑]** to recall the DOS Shell command or type **DOSSHELL** and press **[Enter]**.

② Press **[F10]** and press **[→]** three times to highlight Tree. Press **[Enter]** to select Tree and press **[↓]** two times to highlight Expand All. Then press **[Enter]** to expand the directory structure. If you are using the mouse, click **Tree** then click **Expand All**. Now you can see the directories below CASHFLOW.

③ Press **[Tab]** to move to the Directory Tree window. Press **[↓]** five times to highlight the directory named SUMMARY, under the CASHFLOW directory. If you are using the mouse, click the **SUMMARY** directory.

④ Press **[Del]**, the shortcut key to delete a file or directory. The DOS Shell displays the Deletion Error dialog box. See Figure 3-33. It reports that you *cannot* delete a directory that contains files. You *must* first delete the files. Press **[Enter]** to select Close. If you are using the mouse, click **Close**.

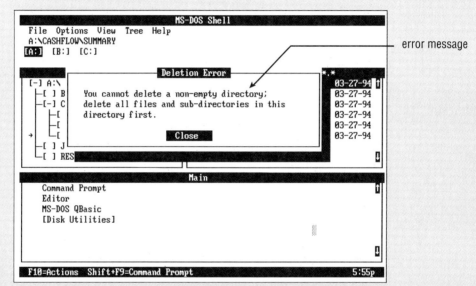

error message

Figure 3-33
The DOS Shell's
Deletion Error
dialog box

⑤ Press **[Tab]** to move to the file list window. If you are using the mouse, click the first file in this window.

⑥ Press **[F10]**, press **[Enter]** to select File, and then type **S** to select all the files in the file list window. If you are using the mouse, click the first filename in the file list window, then press and hold **[Shift]** while you click the last filename, **CASHFLOW.WK1**. The DOS Shell selects all the files.

⑦ Press **[Del]** to delete the files. The DOS Shell displays the Delete File dialog box to verify that you want to delete the files. See Figure 3-34 on the following page. Press **[Enter]** to select OK. If you are using the mouse, click **OK**. The DOS Shell then displays each filename and asks you to verify whether or not you want to delete the file.

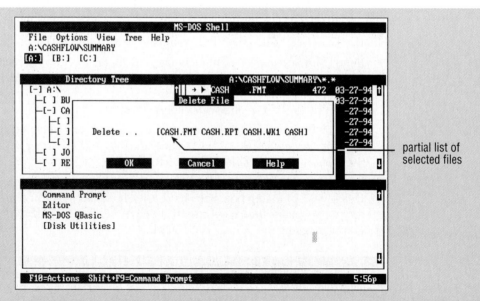

Figure 3-34
The DOS Shell's
Delete File dialog
box prompts for
verification

partial list of
selected files

⑧ Press **[Enter]** to delete each file. If you are using the mouse, click **Yes** to delete each file. After DOS deletes all the files, the dialog box disappears and you return to the Directory Tree window.

Now that you have deleted all the files in the SUMMARY directory, you are ready to delete the directory.

To delete the SUMMARY directory:

① Be sure the SUMMARY directory is still selected.

② Press **[Del]**. The Delete Directory Confirmation dialog box appears. See Figure 3-35. The DOS Shell displays the full path name of the directory. Press **[Enter]**. If you are using the mouse, click **Yes**. The DOS Shell removes the directory and updates the directory tree.

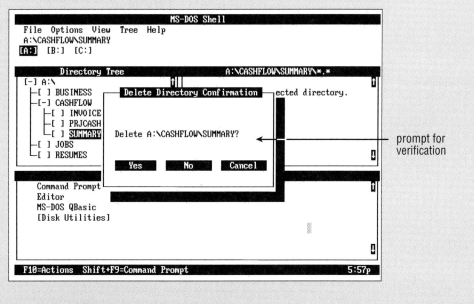

Figure 3-35
The DOS Shell's
Delete Directory
Confirmation
dialog box

❸ Press **[Home]** to return to the root directory. If you are using the mouse, click the root directory.

❹ Press **[F3]** to exit the DOS Shell.

Viewing and Printing a Directory Tree from the DOS Prompt

You want to print a copy of your directory tree and the files contained in each of the directories. If the diskette fails or becomes damaged, you or your business partner will need to reconstruct part or all of the directory structure and restore your business files to the proper directories.

You can use the TREE command to view a directory tree at the DOS prompt. Then you can use a variation of the same command to print a copy of the directory tree.

To display and print the directory tree of your DOS Tutorials diskette:

❶ Be sure the current drive is the one with your DOS Tutorials diskette.

❷ Be sure you are at the root directory. If not, type **CD ** and press **[Enter]**.

❸ Use **[↑]** to recall the DIR/O/P command or type **DIR /O /P** and press **[Enter]**. DOS shows four directories below the root directory. See Figure 3-36 on the following page.

```
A:\>DIR /O /P

 Volume in drive A is BUSINESS
 Volume Serial Number is 0742-18E3
 Directory of A:\

BUSINESS     <DIR>      05-05-94   5:37p
CASHFLOW     <DIR>      05-05-94   5:30p
JOBS         <DIR>      05-05-94   5:43p
RESUMES      <DIR>      05-05-94   5:41p
        4 file(s)              0 bytes
                        671744 bytes free

A:\>
```

Figure 3-36
The directories
below the root
directory

directories

④ Type **TREE** and press **[Enter]**. DOS displays a diagram representing the directory tree. See Figure 3-37. Next to the name of the drive, DOS includes a dot . to indicate that the root directory is the current directory. The directory tree is produced starting at the current directory. This directory tree is similar to the one displayed by the DOS Shell.

root directory

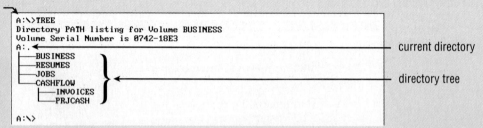

Figure 3-37
The TREE
command displays
the directory tree
structure of your
diskette

```
A:\>TREE
Directory PATH listing for Volume BUSINESS
Volume Serial Number is 0742-18E3
A:.
   ├──BUSINESS
   ├──RESUMES
   ├──JOBS
   └──CASHFLOW
          ├──INVOICES
          └──PRJCASH

A:\>
```

current directory

directory tree

⑤ Type **TREE /F** and press **[Enter]**. With the *Filename switch*, /F, the TREE command displays the directory tree and lists the filenames in each directory. The first part of this directory tree scrolls off the screen.

⑥ Be sure the printer is on, the paper is properly aligned in the printer, and that the printer is on-line.

⑦ Type **TREE /F /A>PRN** and press **[Enter]**. You can redirect the output of any DOS command to the printer by using >PRN. The *ASCII switch*, /A, prints the lines in the directory tree using ASCII or text characters, rather than graphics characters. If your printer can print graphics characters, you can perform this operation without the /A switch.

⑧ If necessary, press the Form Feed button on the printer. If the printer does not respond, press the On Line button to place the printer off-line. Then press Form Feed again. After the printer ejects the page, press the On Line button to place the printer on-line. Figure 3-38 shows the printed copy of the directory tree.

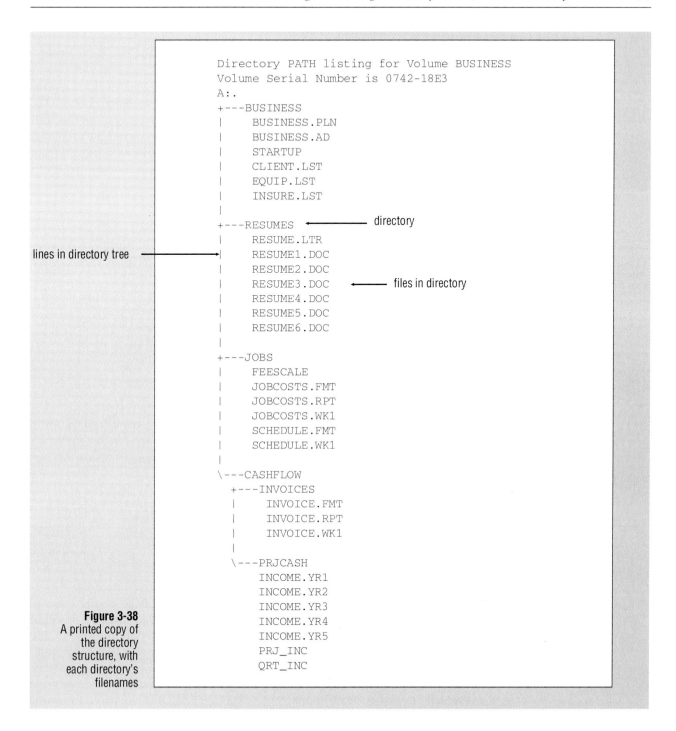

lines in directory tree

directory

files in directory

Figure 3-38
A printed copy of
the directory
structure, with
each directory's
filenames

```
Directory PATH listing for Volume BUSINESS
Volume Serial Number is 0742-18E3
A:.
+---BUSINESS
|     BUSINESS.PLN
|     BUSINESS.AD
|     STARTUP
|     CLIENT.LST
|     EQUIP.LST
|     INSURE.LST
|
+---RESUMES
|     RESUME.LTR
|     RESUME1.DOC
|     RESUME2.DOC
|     RESUME3.DOC
|     RESUME4.DOC
|     RESUME5.DOC
|     RESUME6.DOC
|
+---JOBS
|     FEESCALE
|     JOBCOSTS.FMT
|     JOBCOSTS.RPT
|     JOBCOSTS.WK1
|     SCHEDULE.FMT
|     SCHEDULE.WK1
|
\---CASHFLOW
    +---INVOICES
    |     INVOICE.FMT
    |     INVOICE.RPT
    |     INVOICE.WK1
    |
    \---PRJCASH
          INCOME.YR1
          INCOME.YR2
          INCOME.YR3
          INCOME.YR4
          INCOME.YR5
          PRJ_INC
          QRT_INC
```

The use of the TREE command, or the DOS Shell, to view a directory tree provides you with a quick overview of the directory structure of a disk or diskette. You can use either to locate specific directories and to periodically evaluate the organization of diskettes.

Navigating Within the Directory Tree at the DOS Prompt

In the DOS Shell, you selected and viewed the contents of directories below the CASHFLOW directory by moving the selection cursor in the Directory Tree window. Now, you need to learn how to navigate within the directory tree at the DOS prompt so that you can use both approaches in the day-to-day operations of your business. You already know how to change from the root directory to a directory below the root directory. To test this same process from the DOS prompt, change to the INVOICES directory. This directory is located two levels below the root directory.

To change to the INVOICES directory:

❶ Be sure you are at the root directory of the drive containing your DOS Tutorials diskette.

❷ Type **CD CASHFLOW\INVOICES** and press **[Enter]**. The DOS prompt shows that you are in the INVOICES directory. If you specify the full path name of the directory, you can change to the directory in one step. You could also type CD CASHFLOW to change to the CASHFLOW directory, and then type CD INVOICES to change to the INVOICES directory. However, that approach requires two steps.

Now, you want to move to the CASHFLOW directory — the parent directory of INVOICES.

❸ Type **CD..** and press **[Enter]**. The DOS prompt shows that you are in the CASHFLOW directory. This command tells DOS to move to the directory one level higher in the directory structure of the disk. You can now use the same command to return to the root directory.

❹ Type **CD..** and press **[Enter]**. The DOS prompt now shows that you are in the root directory. Again, you move up one level in the directory tree.

Locating Files with the DIR Command

You need to prepare for a meeting with a business client to discuss a large job that you will do for that client. To do so you need to update a report on job costs, your client list, and your business insurance check list. The job costs report is in a file called JOBCOSTS.RPT. The check lists are in files with the .LST file extension. You can use the DIR command's Subdirectory Search switch to quickly locate the files.

The **Subdirectory Search switch**, **/S**, searches through directories for one or more files. You can look for a single file by name, or you can use wildcards to expand the scope of a search and look for a group of files.

Before you use the DIR command with this switch, you must decide where you want to start the search. In most cases, you will want to return to the root directory and start the search from the top of the directory tree. DOS will search through all the directories, starting with the root directory. If it locates a file or files using the file specification that you provide, it shows the full path name of the file and a directory listing for it, with the filename, size, date, and time. If DOS locates more than one file with the same name, in different directories, it lists each occurrence of the file.

To locate the file named JOBCOSTS.RPT:

① Type **DIR JOBCOSTS.RPT** (without the /S switch) and press **[Enter]**. DOS reports that it found no file by that name. Because you did not include the /S switch, DOS limited its search to the files in the root directory. It did not search the directories below the root directory.

② Press **[F3]** to repeat the last DOS command. Then press **[Space]**, type **/S** and press **[Enter]**. DOS locates the file in the JOBS directory. See Figure 3-39.

filename

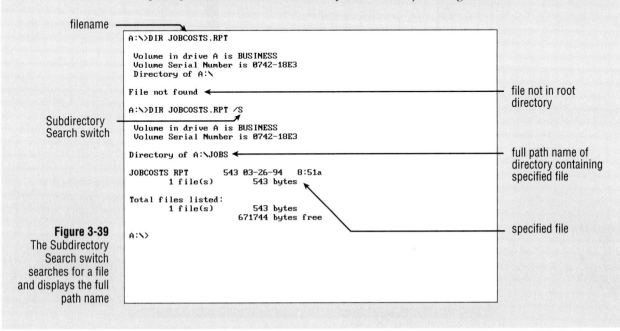

Subdirectory
Search switch

Figure 3-39
The Subdirectory
Search switch
searches for a file
and displays the full
path name

file not in root
directory

full path name of
directory containing
specified file

specified file

```
A:\>DIR JOBCOSTS.RPT

 Volume in drive A is BUSINESS
 Volume Serial Number is 0742-18E3
 Directory of A:\

File not found

A:\>DIR JOBCOSTS.RPT /S

 Volume in drive A is BUSINESS
 Volume Serial Number is 0742-18E3

 Directory of A:\JOBS

JOBCOSTS RPT         543 03-26-94    8:51a
             1 file(s)        543 bytes

Total files listed:
             1 file(s)         543 bytes
                          671744 bytes free

A:\>
```

For comparison, you decide to use the DOS Shell to locate the next file. You have discovered that the DOS Shell provides a more friendly and visual interface for viewing the results of file and disk operations.

To use the DOS Shell to locate the file named CLIENT.LST:

① Use **[↑]** to recall the DOSSHELL command or type **DOSSHELL** and press **[Enter]**.

② Press **[F10]** and press **[→]** three times to highlight Tree. Press **[Enter]** to select Tree and press **[↓]** twice to highlight Expand All. Then, press **[Enter]** to expand the directory structure. If you are using the mouse, click **Tree** then click **Expand All**. Now you can see the directories below CASHFLOW.

③ Press **[F10]**. Press **[Enter]** to select the File menu, press **[↓]** four times to highlight the Search command, then press **[Enter]**. If you are using the mouse, click **File** then click **Search**. The DOS Shell displays the Search File dialog box. See Figure 3-40 on the following page. The cursor is placed in the text box where you specify the file you want to search for.

Figure 3-40
The DOS Shell's
Search File
dialog box

④ Be sure the box labeled "Search entire disk" contains an "X." If this check box is empty, press **[Tab]** and then press **[Space]**. To return to the text box, press **[Shift][Tab]**. If you are using the mouse, click the box next to "Search entire disk," then click in the "Search for" text box.

⑤ Type ***.LST**, then press **[Enter]** If you are using the mouse, click **OK**. The DOS Shell displays another screen with an alphabetical list of files that meet this specification. See Figure 3-41. It also shows the full path name of each file.

Figure 3-41
DOS Shell locates
and displays the
full path names of
all files with the
file extension LST

⑥ Press **[Esc]** to exit this screen view.

⑦ Press **[F3]** to exit the DOS Shell.

Congratulations on successfully completing the tutorials that introduced you to DOS and its basic commands and features. The next section covers the use of a new feature in DOS 6.0. If you are using DOS 5.0, you should read the next section, but you will not be able to complete the steps. This information might help you decide whether or not to upgrade to DOS 6.0.

Checking for Computer Viruses with DOS 6.0

Your business partner has just found a computer virus on a data diskette. **Computer viruses** are programs that damage or adversely affect the performance of a computer system. Your partner recommends that you check your diskettes immediately. Most computer viruses are transferred from one computer system to another by exchanging diskettes. Currently, there are over 1,000 known computer viruses that affect computer systems in different ways. Two or three new viruses are discovered each week.

Because computer viruses can spread rapidly from one computer system to another via infected diskettes, you must frequently check your diskettes and hard disk for the appearance of computer viruses. Many computer systems and networks are set up so that an anti-viral program automatically checks for the presence of viruses when the computer systems are turned on.

DOS 6.0 includes a new feature that checks directories for the presence of computer viruses. This program, called **Microsoft Anti-Virus**, is easy to use. If Microsoft Anti-Virus locates a virus that it recognizes, it can eliminate the virus from the diskette or disk. If it does not recognize a virus, then the virus is either a newly introduced virus or one that the program is not able to detect.

To check your DOS Tutorials diskette for computer viruses:

1. Be sure the current drive is the one with your DOS Tutorials diskette. If necessary, change drives.

2. At the DOS prompt, type **MSAV** and press **[Enter]**. The Microsoft Anti-Virus Main Menu appears. See Figure 3-42 on the following page. *MSAV* is an abbreviation for Microsoft Anti-Virus. The Main Menu contains five options. Note that your screen view might be slightly different if you are using graphics mode rather than text mode.

currently selected
menu option

function key
commands

Figure 3-42
The Microsoft
Anti-Virus
Main Menu

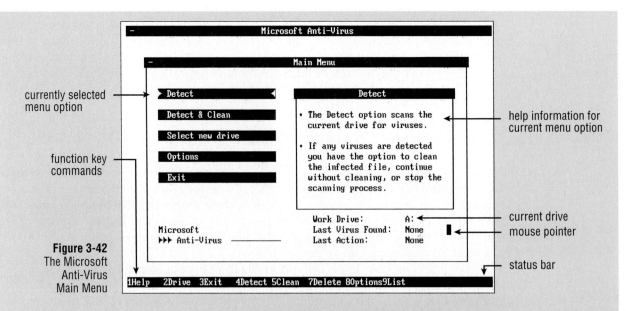

help information for
current menu option

current drive
mouse pointer

status bar

❸ Press [↓] to select the second option, Detect & Clean. This option checks for computer viruses and eliminates any that it finds.

❹ Press **[Enter]**. If you are using the mouse, click **Detect & Clean**. Microsoft Anti-Virus
first checks the computer's memory (RAM) for viruses. Computer viruses load
themselves into memory once they gain access to a computer system. After
Microsoft Anti-Virus checks memory, it checks the files in each directory on your
diskette. The full path names of the files are listed in the upper-left corner as the
program checks each file. Then it displays a screen with its findings. This screen,
titled "Viruses Detected and Cleaned," shows the types of disks and types of files
that the program checked. COM and EXE files are program files with the file extensions COM (for Command File) and EXE (for Executable File). No viruses were
detected on your diskette.

❺ Press **[Enter]** to select OK. If you are using the mouse, click **OK**. The Main Menu
appears.

❻ Press [↓] three times to select the last option, Exit and press **[Enter]**. If you are using
the mouse, click **Exit**. The Close Microsoft Anti-Virus dialog box appears.

❼ Press **[Enter]** to select OK. If you are using the mouse, click **OK**. DOS displays the
DOS prompt.

Now you have another important tool for maintaining the integrity of your files and for
preventing damage to your computer system.

Summary

In this tutorial, you learned how to work with directories from the DOS prompt and from the DOS Shell. You created directories with the MD, or Make Directory, command at the DOS prompt and with the File/Create Directory command in the DOS Shell. You learned how to navigate from one directory to another with the use of the CD, or Change Directory, command at the DOS prompt and by selecting directories from the DOS Shell.

You used the COPY command and the DOS Shell to move files from one directory to another. You used the DIR command and the DOS Shell to display the contents of directories. You removed a directory with the RD, or Remove Directory, command after first deleting all the files in the directory with the DEL command. You also used the DOS Shell to remove a directory after you moved all the files. You used the DIR command and the DOS Shell to locate one or more files by performing a search through the directory structure of a disk.

You viewed the directory tree of your Data Diskette from the DOS Shell. You also displayed and printed a directory tree from the DOS prompt with the TREE command. You used the CD.. command to navigate in the directory tree at the DOS prompt.

Command Reference	
DOS Commands	
CD [directory] or CHDIR [directory]	An internal command that changes from one directory to another
CD ..	An internal command that changes to the directory above the current directory
**CD **	An internal command that changes from the current directory to the root directory
DIR [filename] /S	An internal command that searches through directories for files, and displays a list of filenames with the full path name of the directory where the files are stored
MD [directory] or MKDIR [directory]	An internal command that creates, or makes, a directory
RD [directory] or RMDIR [directory]	An internal command that removes a directory after all the files in the directory have been moved or deleted, provided the directory is not the current directory
TREE	An external command that displays a diagram of the directory tree
DOS Shell Commands	
File/Create Directory	Creates a directory
File/Move	Moves one or more files to another directory
File/Search	Searches through directories for a file or files
File/Select All	Selects all the files listed in the file list window
Tree/Expand All	Expands the directory tree to show all directories

Questions

Use your DOS Exercises diskette to assist you with these questions.   *[handwritten: mD TOOLS ↵]*

1. What command would you use to create a directory named TOOLS below the root directory? What command would you use next to create a directory named WP51 below TOOLS?   *[handwritten: CD TOOLS ↵   mD WP51 ↵]*

2. What command would you use to change from the root directory to a directory named TOOLS? What command would you use next to change to a directory named WP51 below TOOLS?   *[handwritten: CD TOOLS ↵   CD WP51 ↵   DIr ↵]*

3. What command would you use to change from a directory named TOOLS\WP51 to the root directory?   *[handwritten: CD \ ↵]*

4. List two commands that you could use to change from a directory named TOOLS\WP51 to the directory named TOOLS.   *[handwritten: CD.. ↵   CD\TOOLS ↵]*

5. How do you move files from one directory to another at the DOS prompt?   *[handwritten: Source to target]*

6. You have a directory named OLDFORMS below the root directory, and you want to remove this directory. Assume this directory contains files. What command(s) would you use to remove this directory?   *[handwritten: rd Oldforms ↵   Del ↵]*

7. What command would you enter to display a directory tree from the root directory?   *[handwritten: tree ↵]*

8. You want to locate a file named 93TAXES.REC. What command would you enter from the root directory to check all subdirectories so that you could find this file?   *[handwritten: DIR A:\93TAXES.REC /O/S/PE ↵]*

9. How would you create a directory named CREDIT below the root directory in the DOS Shell?

10. How would you change from the root directory to another directory named CREDIT\CARDS in the DOS Shell?

11. How would you move files from a directory named CARDLIST to another named CREDIT\CARDS in the DOS Shell?

12. How can you control the display of the directory tree in the DOS Shell?

13. After you move, delete, and copy files in the DOS Shell, how can you update the file lists for each directory?

[handwritten in left margin: refresh   screen   F5]

CD\MARKETS.   MD FUTURE

14. Suppose you have a directory named MARKETS on drive C. If this directory is below the main directory of drive C, what command would you enter at the DOS prompt to change to the MARKETS directory? If there is a directory named FUTURE below MARKETS, what command would you enter to change to that directory? What command would you enter to return to the root directory of drive C in one step? *CD*

15. Suppose you have a directory named BENEFITS on drive C. This directory is below the root directory of drive C. What command would you enter at the DOS prompt to display an alphabetical list of the files in the BENEFITS directory from the root directory of drive C? *CD Benefits ↵ Dir↵*

16. Suppose you have a directory named OLDFILES in which you temporarily store unused files. This directory is below the root directory of drive C. You decide to delete the OLDFILES directory. What two commands would you enter at the DOS prompt to remove this directory and its files?

17. Suppose you have a directory named BIDS below the main directory and another directory named 1994 below the one named BIDS. Assume these subdirectories are located on drive C. What is the full path name of the directory BIDS? What is the full path name of the directory 1994? What command would you enter at the DOS prompt to change from the root directory to the 1994 directory in one step? What command would you enter to change to its parent directory? *C:\BIDS>   C:\BIDS\1994>*
CD BIDS\1994 ↵   CD..↵

18. You currently are in a directory named PROJECTS. Its full path name is C:\PROJECTS. You want to change to a directory named RECORDS. Its full path name is C:\RE-CORDS. List the command(s) you would use to change directories from the DOS prompt. Assume drive C is the current drive. *CD RECORDS↵*

19. Assume you want to copy all the files in the directory C:\CONTRACT to the directory C:\TRAINING. What command would you enter at the DOS prompt to perform this operation from the root directory? Assume drive C is the current drive.
COPY C:\CONTRACT. C:\TRAINING↵*

20. Assume you have just created a new directory named C:\WPFILES. You want to copy all the files from the root directory with the file extension DOC to this new directory. What command would you enter at the DOS prompt to perform this operation?
Copy C:*.DOC C:\WPFILES↵

21. You keep all your work files in a directory named C:\WORK. The number of files in this directory now exceeds 50. You want to create a new directory named C:\MEMOS and copy all the files with the file extension MEM from the directory C:\WORK to C:\MEMOS. Then, you want to delete those files from C:\WORK. List the steps and commands that you would use to accomplish this operation from the DOS prompt. Assume you are working at the root directory of drive C.

22. You are working in the file list window of the DOS Shell. The DOS Shell is displaying the files in the root directory. You want to move all of these files to a directory named LETTERS. List the steps that you would follow to perform this operation.

MD MEMOS ↵
*copy c:\ *.MEM c:\memos ↵*
*Del *.mem ↵*

23. You are working in the file list window of the DOS Shell. You want to select another directory, one named PAYROLL, so that you can view the files in that directory. List the steps that you would follow to change to this directory.

24. What command would you enter at the DOS prompt to locate a file named 93BUDGET.DOC on drive C? Assume that you are working at the root directory of drive C and that the file could be stored in any of the directories on drive C.

25. What command would you enter at the DOS prompt to locate all the budget document files on drive C for the last three years? Assume the files begin with two digits for the year — 91, 92, and 93 — and that you are working at the root directory of drive C.

26. What command would you enter at the DOS prompt to locate all the tax records on drive C for the last three years? Assume the files all have the file extension .REC and that you are working in the directory named C:\EARNINGS.

27. After you power on your computer system, the DOS prompt appears as C>. You want to change the prompt so that you can see the full path name of each directory as you change from one directory to another. What command can you enter at the DOS prompt so that the DOS prompt shows the full path name? Assume you are working at the root directory of drive C. After you enter this command, what does the DOS prompt look like?

28. When you view a directory listing of a directory, you see two files — one named dot (.) and the other named dot dot (..). What do these two files represent?

29. What is a parent directory?

30. Assume you are working in a directory named DOSCLASS, which is stored on a data diskette. Also assume this directory is below the root directory. List two commands that you can enter at the DOS prompt to change from the DOSCLASS directory to the root directory.

Tutorial Assignments

1. **Displaying the Files in a Directory**: Use your *DOS Tutorials diskette* to perform the following operations from the DOS prompt. List the command that you use to accomplish each step:
   a. Display an alphabetical list of all files in the directory named BUSINESS, one screen at a time.
   b. Display an alphabetical list of all files in all directories that have filenames with the file extension RPT, one screen at a time.
   c. Display an alphabetical list of all files in all directories that have WK as the first two characters of the file extension, one screen at a time.
   d. Display an alphabetical list of all files in all directories, one screen at a time.

2. **Creating Directories at the DOS Prompt**: Use the *DOS Exercises diskette* to perform the following operations from the root directory. List the command that you use to accomplish each step.
   a. Create a directory named CLIENTS below the root directory.
   b. Change to the CLIENTS directory.
   c. Create a directory named REPORTS below the CLIENTS directory.
   d. Create a directory named PROJECTS below the CLIENTS directory.
   e. Create a directory named BIDS below the root directory.
   f. Change to the root directory and display a directory tree.
   g. Print the directory tree.

3. **Creating and Copying Directories at the DOS Prompt**: Use the *DOS Exercises diskette* to perform the following operations from the DOS prompt. List the command that you use to accomplish each step.
   a. From the root directory, create a directory named DOCUMENT below the root directory.
   b. Change to the DOCUMENT directory.
   c. Create a directory named RESUMES below the DOCUMENT directory.
   d. Copy all files in the root directory with a file extension of DOC to the RESUMES directory and change the file extension to WP in one step.
   e. Verify the copy operation.
   f. Delete all files in the root directory with the file extension DOC.
   g. Change to the root directory.

4. **Creating Directories from the DOS Shell**: Use the *DOS Exercises diskette* to perform the following operations from the DOS Shell. List the step or steps for each of these operations.
   a. Create a directory named 123FILES below the root directory.
   b. Move all the files in the root directory with the file extension WK1 and FMT to the directory named 123FILES.
   c. Change the name of the directory 123FILES to FORECAST.
   d. Create another directory named FINANCES below the root directory.
   e. Change to the directory FINANCES and create a directory named CASHFLOW below FINANCES.
   f. Move all the files in the root directory that have CASH as the last four characters of an eight-character filename to the directory named CASHFLOW.
   g. Refresh the screen and verify the move operations.
   h. Change to the root directory and then exit the DOS Shell.

5. **Reorganizing the Directory Structure of a Disk with the DOS Shell**: Make a copy of your DOS Tutorials diskette. Then, apply the concepts and features that you learned in this tutorial to reorganize the directories on the diskette with the use of the DOS Shell. List the step or steps for each of the following operations.

    a. Make a copy of your DOS Tutorials diskette and label the diskette "Challenge Assignment."

    b. Create a directory named LISTS below the root directory.

    c. Move all files with the file extension LST from the directory named BUSINESS to the LISTS directory.

    d. Create directories named INVOICES and PRJCASH below the root directory.

    e. Move the files in CASHFLOW\INVOICES to \INVOICES. Then move the files in CASHFLOW\PRJCASH to \PRJCASH.

    f. Remove the directories named INVOICES and PRJCASH below the CASHFLOW directory. Then remove the CASHFLOW directory.

    g. Refresh the screen and verify the move operations.

    h. Change to the root directory.

    i. Exit the DOS Shell and, from the DOS prompt, print a complete directory tree with filenames.

DOS v5.0/6.0 Tutorials Index